"Religious doubt exists at epidemic levels today, and it is usually not primarily factual or intellectual in nature. As a result, we need books on this topic like this one by Bobby Conway. Many of us require a 'Doubt GPS' to lead us stealthily through the twists, turns, and even the drop-offs. And just as doubt comes from many different angles, so it was wonderful to see the multitude of insights, suggestions, and even remedies that are found in this text, all at different levels, as well. On top of everything else, this volume is well-written—a quick read. If you know Bobby, you're probably not surprised. I suggest that you take a look and see the suggestions for yourself, a loved one, or a friend who may be going through a painful process."—**Gary R. Habermas**, distinguished research professor and chair, philosophy department, Liberty University and Theological Seminary

"Bobby Conway has written an immensely practical, well-informed, and much-needed book on doubt. It deserves a wide readership, as it addresses a significant—though often neglected—concern in many Christian circles."—**Paul Copan**, professor of philosophy and ethics and the Pledger Family Chair, Palm Beach Atlantic University

"If you're agonizing from the deleterious effects of doubting your faith, let me offer up a remedy. Read Bobby Conway's *Doubting Toward Faith*." —**William Lane Craig**, research professor of philosophy, Talbot School of Theology

"In an era in which Internet distortions travel halfway around the world before truth has had a chance to put its boots on, doubt is as common as rust and, left unresolved, equally corrosive. Bobby Conway exhorts us to be skeptical of our doubts and to relentlessly pursue God in the midst of them. Application of the principles in this timely boo the specter of debilitating doubt to definitive devotedness Christ."—**Hank Hanegraaff**, president of the Christian tute and author of numerous books, including *AfterLife: W. Know about Heaven, the Hereafter, and Near-Death Experie*

"Bobby Conway shows how God can use our spiritual questions to lead us to a more confident faith in Christ. Drawing on a wealth of biblical insight, expert opinion, and hard-earned experience, Conway will help you address your own doubts—while learning how to help friends work through theirs."—**Mark Mittelberg**, bestselling author of *Confident Faith* and *The Questions Christians Hope No One Will Ask (With Answers)*

"Bobby Conway has been responding to doubt and skepticism for years as the host of the One Minute Apologist. In *Doubting Toward Faith*, he has given us a valuable tool to help those who have been injured by doubt and those who seek to use their doubt to energize their own spiritual journey. Bobby defines the various forms of doubt, examines specific doubts particular to Christianity, and then provides a roadmap toward clarity, peace, and confidence. If you're struggling with doubt, or know someone who is, this book is a godsend."—**J. Warner Wallace**, cold-case detective and author of *Cold-Case Christianity* and *God's Crime Scene*

"Bobby Conway shows you the causes of doubt, the solutions to doubt, the benefits of doubt, and why you should start doubting your doubts. This encouraging book will have you realizing that it takes too much faith to believe anything other than Christianity."—**Frank Turek**, author of *Stealing from God* and coauthor of *I Don't Have Enough Faith to Be an Atheist*

"Choosing our worldview is perhaps the most important decision an individual will ever make, since one's destiny in life and eternity may be determined in the process. It is only normal, therefore, to second-guess or have doubts pertaining to the wisdom of our choice. For those of us who are often tortured with doubt, Bobby Conway brings hope and guidance!" —**Michael Licona**, PhD, associate professor of theology, Houston Baptist University

DOUBTING
TOWARD
FAITH

BOBBY CONWAY

HARVEST HOUSE PUBLISHERS
EUGENE, OREGON

Cover by Dual Identity, Inc, Whites Creek, Tennessee

Published in association with William K. Jensen Literary Agency, 119 Bampton Court, Eugene, Oregon 97404.

DOUBTING TOWARD FAITH

Copyright © 2015 Bobby Conway
Published by Harvest House Publishers
Eugene, Oregon 97402
www.harvesthousepublishers.com

Library of Congress Cataloging-in-Publication Data
   Conway, Bobby, 1973-
   Doubting toward faith / Bobby Conway.
     pages cm
   ISBN 978-0-7369-6354-1 (pbk.)
   ISBN 978-0-7369-6355-8 (eBook)
   1. Faith. I. Title.
   BT771.3.C67 2015
   234'.23—dc23

2015004704

Printed in the United States of America

15 16 17 18 19 20 21 22 23 / VP-JH / 10 9 8 7 6 5 4 3 2 1

To my dear friend and fellow elder, Matt Hatfield.

I can't imagine life without your friendship.
You've stood by my side through a hundred trials and more.
And when doubts brought me despair,
you quietly and wisely helped carry me through.
I'll forever be grateful.

Acknowledgments

Thanks to...

My beloved wife and children: Heather, Haley, and Dawson. Thank you for your support and encouragement through writing this book. You guys are the best.

My fellow elders and staff. Oh, how I love serving the Lord with you. I could never do all this alone. Together is definitely better.

Harvest House Publishers for your passion to publish a book designed to provide hope for hopeless doubters.

Jeff Kinley, Rod Morris, Bennett Harris, Gary Habermas, and Christian Research Institute for your editorial help and creative insights. You guys helped bring this all together. I so appreciate you.

Bill Jensen, my literary agent, for believing in this book. You've opened so many doors for me. For that, I'll always be indebted.

Sean McDowell for championing *Doubting Toward Faith* by writing a gracious foreword.

William Lane Craig for your overwhelming influence on my life. Your books, podcasts, debates, and ministry have shaped the way I think about many subjects, including doubt. Your scholarship is so appreciated.

The Lord Jesus Christ for never leaving us or forsaking us—even through our darkest doubts, You're always there.

CONTENTS

Foreword by Sean McDowell 9

1. A Crisis of Doubt 13

2. A Splinter in the Mind 31

3. Jesus Can Handle Your Doubts 49

4. Doubt Triggers: Part 1 69

5. Doubt Triggers: Part 2 91

6. Four Facets of Doubt 111

7. The Root of Doubt 133

8. Navigating Doubt 153

9. Faith Defined 177

10. *Toward* Faith 191

Appendix—Two Extra Tips
for Navigating Doubt 205

Notes 207

FOREWORD

By Sean McDowell

Doubting *Toward Faith* is a refreshing book. It made me laugh. It made me cry. And yet it also made me upset. Why? Because I wish this book had existed years ago when I went through my own period of substantial doubt. Even though I have been blessed with amazing friends and family during my entire journey of faith, this book would have been life-giving when I first began to seriously doubt my own beliefs. The insights Bobby shares would have saved me a lot of heartache and given me a helpful roadmap for navigating the world of doubt and faith.

My doubts first hit as a college student. Before this period in my life, my faith was simply something I took for granted. I have fond memories of attending Christian conferences, going on mission trips, and listening to my father as he taught the Bible. My parents raised me in the Christian faith. As a child growing up, I can never remember *not* believing in the Christian story of the world.

Yet as a college student, I felt the gravity of my beliefs for the first time. What if I were raised in a different family? Is Jesus really the only way to God? How do I know Christianity is true? Sometimes these doubts were so intense they felt paralyzing. I decided to share these doubts with my dad, who has (now) been an evangelist and apologist for over five decades.

His response completely took me by surprise. "I think it's great that you want to find truth," he said. "It's wise not to simply accept things just because you were told them. You need to find out if Christianity is true. You know that your mom and I love you regardless of what you conclude. Seek after truth and take to heart the things your mom and I have taught you. Reject what you have learned growing up only if you believe it is not true."

As I look back on this experience, now that I am a speaker and apologist myself, I have learned a few key things about doubt. First, doubts don't have to be the end of faith. In fact, doubts can often be the impetus for the development of a deeper, more genuine faith. This has certainly been true in my life. But this doesn't happen by accident. It is important to take the kinds of steps that you will find in *Doubting Toward Faith*.

Second, don't doubt alone. As Bobby points out multiple times, be sure to share your doubts with others. When you are in the middle of doubting, it is critical to experience the love, grace, and guidance of the body of Christ. Doubting alone is a recipe for disaster. I thank God for the people who loved me and guided me through my season of doubt.

Third, use your doubts as a motivator for learning. Sometimes I envy those who have the faith of a child and never seem to doubt. I used to be hard on myself until I realized that my questions and doubts often drive me to understand. If I had a simple faith, then I wouldn't be as motivated to study intelligent design, the historical Jesus, or tough ethical issues. I wouldn't have the same hunger for knowledge. And yet I have learned to thank God for the people with simple faith, for they use their gift to encourage the body of Christ.

The reality of doubt has been ignored for too long in the church. With our age of unlimited information and endless truth-claims, people will inevitably experience doubt. Rather than seeing this as a bad thing, I pray the church will see this as an opportunity to help people go deeper in their faith.

And that is why I am thankful for *Doubting Toward Faith*. Bobby Conway honestly and insightfully probes the reality of doubt, but also provides hopeful and practical ways forward. I think you will enjoy the journey.

Sean McDowell, PhD, assistant professor
Biola University

Chapter 1

A CRISIS OF DOUBT

"For those with faith, no explanation is necessary.
For those without, no explanation is possible."

THOMAS AQUINAS

"It is not as a child that I believe and confess Jesus Christ.
My hosanna is born of a furnace of doubt."

FYODOR DOSTOYEVSKY

This is a book about doubt. Beyond surpassing wonder about God or mere inquiry about Him and His truth, doubt digs much deeper. Doubt doesn't just ask, "What is real?" It poses the challenge, "Is my *faith* real?" Is what I believe really valid? Or is it simply a modified myth, an uber-marketed religious fairy tale supported by millions of gullible minds throughout history?

Doubt trumps wondering, and it body-slams mere curiosity. In its *worst* form, it goes beyond simply searching for answers to questions, inevitably denying the legitimacy of the questions themselves.

Doubt can drive us to seek truth or it can drown us in despair, hopelessness, and confusion.

For Christians, doubt can either serve us or sink us. It can drive us to seek truth or it can drown us in despair, hopelessness, and confusion. If ignored or left unchecked, it can bore into our brain, releasing a virus of unbelief, infecting and eventually destroying every healthy thought about God. It can take us to the place where nothing else matters. Where we find ourselves loathing even life itself.

If left unchecked, intellectual doubt metastasizes, seeping its way into our emotions and collecting a wide array of fears, worries, anxieties, anger, confusion, depression, and ultimately despair at the thought of being played or duped or envisioning a life without our once "cherished belief" in God.

A World in Transition

That's why I wrote this book—to keep you from ever getting to that breaking point or to help you if you're already there. I'm going to show you how to look your doubts squarely in the eyes and stare them down. Together, we'll examine the sources, causes, and kinds of doubts. You may ask, "Do we really need a whole book on doubt? Is this really a huge issue in the church today?" In a word, yes, it really is. It's a bigger issue than most Christians realize.

Capturing the zeitgeist of our changing times is quite the project. We live in a multitextured culture that is replete with innumerable beliefs, opinions, ideas, and life philosophies. Ours is a culture of doubt and longing, faith and questioning, searching and probing. And much of the doubt has been accelerated by fast-paced change. Our culture is living between the tension of what we once were and what we are now becoming. And for many, waiting in the blank space between the definition of what we were and the search to define what we are becoming feels for the moment confusing, and even a bit uncomfortable.

Echoing this angst, Os Guinness writes, "We live in an age of doubt, disillusion and disaffiliation, which naturally prizes what has been described as 'the faith that you go to when you don't know where to go.'"[1] Both our pluralistic and secularized culture has produced a fragilized-self as it pertains to doubt.[2] We've shifted from Christianity to *Anyanity* (pluralism) or *Noanity* (atheism).

Belief isn't nearly as comfortable and cozy as it once seemed. There's an irritant to it; like a pebble in a shoe, these competing beliefs have made the faith walk a little less comfortable. Today, record numbers of those who once professed faith in Christ are walking away from the church, even limping, *in the name of doubt.* I believe the church is more threatened by doubt today than at any time in her two thousand years of existence.

> Belief isn't nearly as comfortable
> and cozy as it once seemed.

External Threats

Our faith faces threats from the outside. Many New Atheists have sought to supplant belief in transcendence altogether. Number one on the agenda is an attempt to jettison God once and for all. Age-old questions are being repackaged, setting off alarms in the hearts of many believers. Publications from these fundamentalist atheist writers work in unison, raining a downpour of doubt on believers and unbelievers alike. Books such as Richard Dawkins's highly acclaimed *The God Delusion*, or Sam Harris's *The End of Faith*, or Daniel Dennett's *Breaking the Spell*, or the late Christopher Hitchens's *God Is Not Great: How Religion Poisons Everything* have created for many an insurmountable mountain of doubt, causing some believers to secretly ask, "Could this universe be all there is?"

These New Atheists are determined to create unbelief in believers, even employing the use of billboards that read, "Millions of people are happy without God, are you?" To many atheists, perhaps God was a useful fiction to serve those on the evolutionary trajectory toward a more modern age of scientific enlightenment. But now that we are enlightened, the time has come, once and for all, to bury heaven's so-called architect—God. *We* are the architects.

Friedrich Nietzsche's famed "God is dead" mantra is still widely circulated, but so is this inescapable, inner-inkling whereby much of mankind still wonders if there is something or Someone *beyond* the universe—something even transcendent. Something like…God. So, the tables can be turned. Even the honest atheist has his moments where he asks himself, "Could I be wrong? Does…*He* exist?"

It turns out that neither belief nor unbelief comes easy in a world as eclectic as this place we call home. Nevertheless, many atheists, and especially the New Atheists, seek to bury their "what if" questions, holding fast to their predetermined commitment to materialism.

....

Neither belief nor unbelief comes easy in a
world as eclectic as this place we call home.

....

Now to be fair, atheists aren't alone in their attempt to bury God. Others outside of atheism have joined the campaign to end Christian belief. Those like *New York Times* bestselling author Bart Ehrman have contributed to this onslaught of doubt through the release of books such as *How Jesus Became God; Misquoting Jesus;* and *Jesus, Interrupted.* Further, the Muslim Reza Aslan and his book *Zealot: The Life and Times of Jesus of Nazareth* heighten this mountain of doubt among some believers. Adding to this confusion are bloggers who pollute the blogosphere with just enough information to be dangerous. Their empty rhetoric somehow manages to mislead ill-equipped Christians, casting them over the cliff and into the sea of doubt.

Joining this doubt parade is a high-speed moral devolution. Once held values have slipped down the slope into degradation. Here's how this works. Ours was once a culture that *rejected* same-sex marriage. It then *tolerated* the idea. Then *accepted* it. Now it not only *celebrates* same-sex marriage, it *rejects* those who see marriage any other way. This creates great cultural confusion.

Some Christians privately wonder, "Is morality relative after all?" But as Flannery O'Connor would remind us, "Truth does not change according to our ability to stomach it." Cultures morally devolve as they slide down the moral slope in fivefold fashion from rejection, to tolerance, to acceptance, to celebration, and to rejecting the opposite of the very thing they once rejected. Many regard this as cultural progression rather than regression. This creates confusion and doubt.

This moral devolution is traveling at high speed. To prove my point above, state by state, same-sex marriage is being condoned and legalized. By the release date of this book, the Supreme Court will have met again to discuss the national legalization of same-sex marriage, and it's quite possible the verdict as you read this book has already been declared—*Same-sex marriage is now legal in all fifty states*.

The culture is changing with such rapidity that some of my statements in this chapter are probably in need of a little freshening up. Books designed for school-age children with titles like *Jacob's New Dress* or *When Kayla Was Kyle* or *Heather Has Two Mommies* have joined the fight to cast doubt on biblical truths, values, and morals.

The gender issue is in such a confused state that some are posing the question, "What's your PGP?" (Your *preferred gender pronoun*.) Some even advocate caution when using the pronouns *he* and *she* because that may not be someone's PGP. California became the first state to allow transgender kids K-12 to pick the bathroom of their preferred gender. In the same state, these students are also allowed to pick which sports teams to play on—the boys' or the girls'.

Adding to the sweeping change, marijuana's legalization is quickly gaining ground. Normalizing what was once forbidden is now old news. And if you don't join the party quickly, you just might taste a little condemnation yourself. The speed at which the culture is changing morally is almost too fast for the church to even process. And as a result, some Christians sadly ask, "Is our God out of touch? Outdated? Does our faith *work* in today's world?"

Some are ready to repackage God, claiming, "It's time to renovate God or remove Him altogether." Even some pastors and writers have sought to give God a facelift, making Him more hip, accessible, and viable for a new generation. New times require a new God. And by freshening Him up a bit, doubting Christians hope to quiet their doubts. Or at least ease them.

> Today, pluralism along with secularism
> reigns supreme, even in many
> professing believers' hearts.

Add to all these external voices the part that multiculturalism plays. Concerning belief, globalization offers a lot of live options. The world is getting smaller, and any number of beliefs are moving in next door, casting a shadow of doubt on the long-cherished view that Jesus is the only way to heaven. Today, pluralism along with secularism reigns supreme, even in many professing believers' hearts. It is becoming harder and harder for Christians to stand united against a chorus of voices crying out against Jesus and His claims. There are even more external threats out there, but I trust you've caught my vibe.

Internal Threats

The church is also threatened from *within*. Many in the church are twisting Scripture to placate the prevailing culture on topics such as hell, homosexuality, gender, abortion, and the exclusivity of Jesus as Savior. To make matters worse, many church leaders are ill-equipped to handle their flock's doubts. Many are so consumed with meetings, programs, buildings, and budgets that "equipping the saints" often becomes an unfortunate afterthought.

Others are so obsessed with being relevant, hip, and marketable that they've failed to help their flocks navigate the truth war before us. And could it be that this fashionable-gospel movement has now created a great harvest field for apostasy to take place by replacing style over substance? And if there's one thing Satan knows about apostasy it's this—doubt precedes apostasy. It always does. Is the church ready to lead this culture of doubt?

....

The church has never been as racked
with doubt as she is today.

....

Sure, the church has given its fair share of how-to messages, but has it equipped the flock how to defend their faith and how to deal with their doubts? My observation and experience tell me that the church has never been as racked with doubt as she is today. I've never seen such an identity crisis within the body of Christ. Never before has Jesus's bride been so confused. And behind much of that confusion lies an irritant called doubt. No longer can pastors, teachers, apologists, and Christian leaders take the easy road and avoid answering the tough questions that plague the average Christian.

Rather, we must engage them.

Wrestle with them.

And defend against them.

Sincere believers, like you, have honest questions that deserve authentic, heartfelt answers. We cannot overlook this fact, especially with our youth, where this crisis of doubt is systemic. Lillian Kwon, in an article about doubt and college kids, writes, "The more college students felt that they had the opportunity to express their doubt while they were in high school, the higher [their] levels of faith maturity and spiritual maturity."[3] Isn't that interesting? David Kinnaman, in his book *You Lost Me,* reinforces this cultural narrative, writing, "I believe unexpressed doubt is one of the most powerful destroyers of faith." This tells us we need to talk about our doubts.

And that conversation must begin in the *church.* The church's role cannot be underestimated as it relates to helping our youth face today's doubt crisis. Church leadership teams everywhere must ask, "How are we going to effectively help not only our youth, but our entire church family navigate their way through today's doubt crisis?" Unfortunately, many churches are passive in this arena. We are often far too detached, too afraid, or too unwilling to deal with people's doubts. And that's a tragedy, because talking about our doubts can prevent us from getting to the place where we are suffocated by our doubts.

> The church's role cannot be
> underestimated as it relates to helping
> our youth face today's doubt crisis.

This conversation also needs to take place *in the home.* Let's face it—children need *permission* to doubt with Mom and Dad. Not only that, they need their parents to be vulnerable enough to share their own doubts, while also teaching their kids how they have sought to handle doubt. This relational capital in the home is paramount for kids. Parents can't force their children to maintain a sanitized faith and stiff-arm their kids for asking thought-provoking questions. If they do, there may be a serious price to pay.

Parents must realize that their kids are going to have their doubts, so why not let them air them out on the home front? Isn't this how it should be? This means parents need to create a safe environment for vulnerable conversations to emerge at the dinner table or wherever. It also means that Mom and Dad need to anticipate today's biggest questions and start learning their stuff. Now is not the time to plug our ears and cover our eyes. Ignoring the battle doesn't change the battle. It just positions us to lose the battle. So gear up. We're at war.

Good Doubt and Bad Doubt

To be clear, not all doubt is bad. Some is good. We should doubt lots of things that aren't true, and having a healthy skeptical attitude can save us from falling prey to a lot of dead-end philosophies. As a Christian, I've examined other beliefs and competing faith systems. Many of these contradict each other and, therefore, they can't all be true. They can all be *wrong*, but since they contradict one another, they can't all be *true*.

....

Not all doubt is bad.

....

So I think it's good to be skeptical and doubt Mormonism. It's good to doubt Islam, to doubt relativism, to doubt atheism, Hinduism, Buddhism, and so on. It's even good to doubt certain things within Christianity. We are not exempt from holding false beliefs. How many Christians (or denominations) do you know who contradict each other? We once believed, along with the rest of the world, that the sun revolved around the earth. It was good to depart from that misguided belief. Doubting other false systems of belief doesn't mean they contain zero truth.[4] It just means that the system as a whole isn't *the* truth. So doubt has its place.

Thinking About Our Faith Versus Doubting Our Faith

There is also a difference between *thinking about our faith* and *doubting our faith*. Thinking about our faith is good, whereas there is a type of doubting our faith that isn't. Doubt is a dark place, and no seeking Christian wants to live in darkness. Doubting shifts from healthy to unhealthy the moment we start doubting the truth. Famed Christian apologist William Lane Craig writes:

When I was an undergraduate at Wheaton College, an attitude was prevalent among the students that doubt was actually a virtue and that a Christian who did not doubt his faith was somehow intellectually deficient or naïve. But such an attitude is unbiblical and confused. It is unbiblical to think of doubt as a virtue; to the contrary, doubt is always portrayed in the Scriptures as something detrimental to spiritual life…how could the students I knew at Wheaton College have got things so totally reversed? It is probably because they had confused *thinking* about their faith with *doubting* their faith. We need to keep the distinction clear.[5]

Craig is right on target here. The Bible doesn't paint doubt in a positive light.[6] While we may need to converse about our doubts, we don't need to celebrate them. There is a difference.

> Doubt must be dealt with lest
> it devastate your faith.

So as I talk about doubt, I'm saying you can't ignore it. It's there. And it must be dealt with lest it devastate your faith. And it starts by understanding how to recognize exactly what doubt is.

Defining Doubt

Resurrection scholar Gary Habermas sheds some helpful light on the meaning of the word *doubt*. The quote is lengthy but well worth the read and even necessary to grasp as we seek our way through this malaise we call doubt.

In the New Testament there are at least a half dozen Greek words that describe the general condition that we have called doubt. They can also have other meanings as well, such as puzzlement or wondering. When used in the sense that is relevant for us, *key meanings include uncertainty or hesitation between two positions*, but there are differences. Interestingly, they are applied to believers and unbelievers alike.

For example, using the most common word for doubt *(diakrino)*, James describes the man who asks God for faith but who wavers concerning whether he thinks God will grant the request. This individual is described as being unsettled (James 1:5-8). Using the same term, Jude instructs believers to have mercy on doubters (Jude 22), who, in the context, were apparently affected by false teachers (vv. 17-23). Matthew mentions that Jesus' followers doubted *(distazo)* him on occasion (14:31; 28:17). In the first instance, Jesus identified Peter as having little faith, and asked him why he doubted. Unbelieving Jews are also described as doubting *(psuchen airo)* Jesus (John 10:24).

Other terms with similar meanings are also used. Paul describes his own condition during times of persecution as being perplexed *(aporeo)*, although he said he did not despair (2 Cor. 4:8). Jesus uses still another word *(meteorizo)* when warning his listeners about anxious worry (Luke 12:29). *Such words regularly indicate a state of vacillation or questioning, even of anxiety, despair, or unbelief.* There is also much variety in the use of these terms, depending on the context. So doubt covers a fairly wide range of possible states of mind, with some diversity regarding the particular situation. It can tend in the direction of unbelief, but it is most commonly used of true believers who lack assurance.[7]

Os Guinness insightfully adds,

> The Latin word for doubt, *dubitare*, comes from an Aryan root meaning "two." To believe or have faith is to be "in one mind" with regard to accepting something as true; to *dis*believe is to be "in one mind" about rejecting it. To doubt is to waver between the two, to believe and doubt at once, and so to be "in two minds."[8]

That's why doubt is so disturbing. *It splits the mind.* Contrary to popular belief, intellectual doubt is *not* the opposite of faith; unbelief is. Doubt is in between, seesawing and dangling in the middle.

Yet, make no mistake. Doubt never stays put. It's not neutral.

It makes up its mind.

It's directional.

It's going somewhere.

This means a person will either doubt toward unbelief or they will doubt toward faith. You'll waver one way or another. Though I recognize that doubt can have broad applications, I'll primarily focus on doubt as it specifically relates to the person with a split mind. To the double-minded Christian.

I'd also add that there is *skeptical* doubt and *sincere* doubt. There is *antagonistic* doubt and *authentic* doubt. And the difference between them is worlds apart. Those who hold to the latter want their doubts solved so they can go forward with God, while the former want their doubts confirmed so they can move *beyond* God.

Don't Panic

So here are my questions for you. Do you ever struggle with doubt regarding your faith, Jesus, the Bible, morality, miracles, or truth? Are you wrestling with your faith and looking for some guidance to effectively face your doubts? Have you ever secretly wondered, "Have I believed a lie? Am I deceived? Could I be wrong?" Have you ever felt like your once "on-fire faith" has lost yesterday's passion? Is the flame just about to go out and you find yourself in that lonely dark place wondering, "God, where are You?" Have you ever felt anxious or even experienced an inner panic as your doubts accumulate?

....
"Faith is the refusal to panic."
....

If so, be encouraged. This book was written for you. As the late Martin Lloyd-Jones, the great British preacher, once said, "Faith is the refusal to panic." That's some sage advice, especially for the Christian threatened by doubts. The lessons you are about to learn will allow you to swap out your panic for peace by showing you a whole new way to doubt.

What is the new way forward in this malaise of confusion that we now live in? Should we go the way of agnostic Vincent Bugliosi, author of *Divinity of Doubt,* who writes, "The whole matter of God can perhaps be distilled down to this. Is there a God who created the world? Or is God a word we use to explain the world? In either event, God should only be a question."[9] According to Bugliosi, the "God question" cannot be answered in the negative or the affirmative.

However, one thing is sure. It's a lot easier to ask questions than it is to find answers. Yet, a life without explanation is exhausting. Therefore, we demand explanation, and fortunately, the Christian worldview comes nicely furnished with explanation. This should give us hope. It also means that now is not the time to throw in the towel.

....

Doubters beware. Doubt is a tireless
nemesis. It must be faced down.

....

Sitting around doubting all the time is a sure way to become self-addicted. It's a recipe for losing sight of God and a guaranteed way to plummet yourself into a melancholic self-absorbed life, whereby everything closes inward, rendering you incapable of seeing outside of your panic-obsessed self. Doubters beware. Doubt is a tireless nemesis. It must be faced down.

Jesus Prevails

It's also helpful to know, as we briefly discussed already, that whenever a culture experiences accelerated change, the door swings open for doubt to creep in and create such panic. However, a brisk walk through the pages of history and it won't be long before you encounter many faithful believers who faced the headwinds of doubt long before our time.

As G.K. Chesterton once wrote, "At least five times...the Faith has to all appearances gone to the dogs. In each of these five cases, it was the dog that died." And Jesus wasn't joking when He said, "I will build my church, and the gates of hell shall *not* prevail against it."[10]

Granted the times are turbulent, but Jesus's words were intentionally cast to create an unwavering confidence that no matter how disoriented life becomes, *He will prevail.* Even if your doubts should weaken you beyond all perceivable hope—still hope. Continue to trust. Don't stop believing. *He will prevail.* As the psalmist once expressed, "When I thought, 'My foot slips,' your steadfast love, O Lord, held me up." Hang on to hope knowing He's hanging on to you. And trust even when it's hard to see.

As every airplane pilot knows, there is such a thing as becoming spatially disoriented. This happens when a pilot is in the clouds and cannot tell if the plane is right-side up or upside down. Talk about scary. In the moment the pilot experiences this confusion, he is faced with a critical choice—trust his feelings or go with the instrument panel. One feels natural and familiar while the other seems detached and foreign. The question that pilot faces is this: "Who's lying and who's telling the truth?" Does he rely on what he senses and what seems real? Or does he go with the instrument panel? Flesh and blood or numbers, lights, and dials? If he wants to be sure, he must look to the attitude direction indicator (ADI), the artificial horizon telling him whether he is up or down. That choice to trust the instrument panel is usually the difference between life and death.

....

We must train ourselves to trust our
instruments. The Christian instruments
are faith and the Word of God.

....

As believers, we may not become spatially disoriented, but we do become *spiritually* disoriented when we are racked with doubts. And like a pilot, we must train ourselves to trust our instruments. The Christian instruments are faith and the Word of God. The Bible is our dependable "direction indicator" and faith helps us to navigate our way through the disorienting clouds of doubt. In the storm of confusion, faith is the direction we aim. And in doubting *toward* faith, we end up doubting toward *God*, the only One who can lead us through the storm and calm our doubts.

As the Christian philosopher Blaise Pascal said, "There is enough light for those who want to believe and enough shadows to blind those who don't." The choice is yours. You can doubt toward unbelief or you can doubt toward faith. The reason we have a doubt crisis today is because there is a faith crisis. You're about to learn the life skill of navigating your doubts toward faith without having to sacrifice your intellect or reason, and in the process, you just might discover the *Truth*.

Interested?

If so, let's get to work.

Doubt Reflections

- *Doubt doesn't just ask, "What is real?" It poses the challenge, "Is my faith real?"*

- *Beware. The church is doubly threatened as it relates to doubt. From both the outside and the inside.*

- *Doubt doesn't stay put. A person will either doubt toward unbelief or they will doubt toward faith.*

Questions for Further Thought and Discussion

1. What stood out to you the most in this chapter?

2. Bobby said the church is more threatened by doubt today than at any time in her two thousand years of existence. Do you agree or disagree with that statement? Explain.

3. Can you think of any historical moments where massive change brought about confusion and doubt? If so, what can we learn from the churches that have stood in our shoes before? Are there any lessons worth discussing?

4. There were several *external threats* mentioned in this chapter to add to today's doubt crisis. Can you think of any others? If not, which ones stood out to you in this chapter?

5. The church is also threatened internally. Does your church have a good plan in place to help doubting Christians or inquisitive nonbelievers to doubt toward faith? If not, how could God use you to help your church be more proactive in aiding hurting doubters?

6. How can parents do a better job in the doubt department with their kids?

Chapter 2

A SPLINTER IN THE MIND

"The beginning of wisdom is found in doubting;
by doubting we come to the question, and by
seeking we may come upon the truth."

PETER ABELARD

"There was a castle called Doubting Castle, the
owner whereof was Giant Despair."

JOHN BUNYAN

For many, she epitomized a life of faith—serving others, inspiring the poor, the needy, and the dying. Few knew the depth of her inner torment, a secret kept for years. Inspiring others for decades toward faith, she questioned her own.

In *Mother Teresa: Come Be My Light,* which contains some of her private letters and journals, we learn that the late Albanian Roman Catholic nun was bombarded by doubt. Like a dark cloud that wouldn't lift, these doubts plagued her until her death in 1997.

Like many today, she felt utterly abandoned by God, even to the point of questioning God's existence. In 1959 she wrote, "If I ever become a saint—I will surely be one of darkness." A few years earlier, she wrote to Archbishop Perier of Calcutta:

> There is so much contradiction in my soul. Such deep longing for God—so deep that it is painful—a suffering continual—and yet not wanted by God—repulsed—empty—no faith—no love—no zeal. Souls hold no attraction—Heaven means nothing—to me it looks like an empty place—the thought of it means nothing to me and yet this torturing longing for God. Pray for me please that I keep smiling at Him in spite of everything. For I am only His—so He has every right over me. I am perfectly happy to be nobody even to God.[1]

This is Mother Teresa *doubting toward faith.* Though stuck in the midst of hopelessness, she nevertheless didn't give up hope. Feeling forsaken, she never forsook God.

"Dear Doubt..."

Have you ever felt this way? Forsaken by God? Lonely? Confused? Depressed? Empty? Fearful? Lifeless? Skeptical? Or even full of questions? Behind the curtain of our doubts reside unanswered questions, such as "How could a loving God allow so much evil and suffering in the world?" Like a river fed by tributaries, this giant mystery is fed by other apparent mysteries that leave us puzzled about our faith:

- God, why did you allow my spouse to die at such a young age?
- Why did my child have to get this incurable leukemia?
- Why are there so many starving children in the world?

Other questions are equally perplexing:

- Can I trust the Bible? Isn't it just man-made and full of contradictions? Hasn't it been changed a lot over the centuries?

- What's the fate of those who have never heard of Jesus?

- Isn't Christianity just a crutch for weak-minded people?

- Does God really exist? If so, does He care about our petty little needs?

- Are miracles still possible?

- Did Jesus really rise from the dead? If so, can I know for sure? How can we prove it?

- Is there such a thing as absolute moral truth? Isn't all truth relative?

- If there is only one God and He is all-loving, surely there are many ways to Him, right?

Why? Why? Why? Like the chorus of a song we cannot get out of our mind, the *why* questions peck incessantly at our mind and spirit. They just won't go away.

If you've ever found yourself asking one or more of these questions, guess what? You're not alone. Let me say that again. You are *not* alone. Any thinker worth his salt has encountered doubts. Every person who engages their mind will find that their faith inevitably wrestles with these doubt-laced questions and paradoxes.

But they're still an annoying nuisance, aren't they? They can twist our life all up, creating turmoil even for the best of believers. Doubt is no respecter of persons. Seasoned saint or hardened sinner, we're all susceptible. We can't hide from doubt, run from it, or ignore it, at least not without consequence. The only thing we can do with our doubts is face them. To look them square in the eye.

> Doubt is no respecter of persons. Seasoned
> saint or hardened sinner, we're all susceptible.

If we fail to do that, doubt will slowly (or sometimes quickly) eat us away, consuming our spiritual energy and draining the blood from our relationship with God. Doubt will strip us of our passion for Christ, rendering us passionless. Ignoring our doubts will not only cause us to live in denial, but also actually feed our doubts, making them grow and fester. Doubt *must* be addressed lest it erode our faith.

And if you're one of the lucky ones who cannot relate to deep doubt, then your responsibility is to help those who do. Remember Jude's exhortation to "have mercy on those who doubt."[2] However, keep in mind that a lack of doubt doesn't necessarily mean you're superspiritual. Many shallow Christians have been spared the agony of doubt because their biblical diet is relegated to a proverb a day. These people don't *live* on the Word; they *snack* on it. And while I'm all for reading the book of Proverbs, it's not until you're faced with real tragedy or dark doubt that you start looking for rock-solid answers.

Never experiencing any level of questioning or doubt may mean you seldom think deeply about faith issues. You may never doubt God's existence, and that's okay. But as a believer living in the twenty-first century filled with skeptics and hostility toward Christianity, you had better have good reason *why* you believe in His existence. Failing to do this results in us being naïve, disconnected, irrelevant, and ineffective in the world to which God has called us to be salt and light.

But for some followers of Jesus, doubt can become utterly pervasive, seeping into our innermost being. Like pulling weeds, we may find ourselves pulling up one doubt after another with the hope of eradicating them once and for all. Yet they remain resilient to our efforts.

Skin Deep or Deeper?

Doubt has been described as a splinter in the mind. It's the sound of a bug you cannot detect, the itch on your back that you cannot scratch, the drip of a faucet you cannot prevent, or the ringing in your ear that you cannot shake. Doubt is a nuisance, to say the least.

With this in mind, what exactly is this uninvited intruder we call doubt? You may be relieved to know that the presence of doubt doesn't mean you aren't a Christian. When we think of doubt, it typically evokes images of atheists like the German philosopher Friederich Nietzsche or perhaps liberal talk show host and comedian Bill Maher.

Remember when you doubt that you're not alone.

It's helpful to remember when you doubt that you're not alone, though I know it often feels that way. However, the Bible as well as history is replete with doubters. Here are a few examples of well-known Christians who have struggled with this splinter called doubt. Sit with them for a moment and listen to their thoughts:

St. Augustine: "Doubt is but another element of faith."

John Calvin: "Surely, while we teach that faith ought to be certain and assured, we cannot imagine any certainty that is not tinged with doubt, or any assurance that is not assailed by some anxiety."[3]

Charles Spurgeon: "I do not believe there ever existed a Christian yet, who did not now and then doubt his interest in Jesus. I think, when a man says, 'I never doubt,' it is quite time for us to doubt him."[4]

C.S. Lewis: "Now that I am a Christian, I do have moods in which the whole thing looks very improbable: but when I was an atheist I had moods in which Christianity looked terribly probable."[5]

Karl Barth: "But in the face of his doubt, even if it be the most radical, the theologian should not despair. Doubt indeed has its time and place. In the present period no one, not even the theologian, can escape it."[6]

Francis Schaeffer: "In 1951 and 1952 I faced a spiritual crisis in my own life...I told [my wife] that for the sake of honesty I had to go all the way back to my agnosticism and think through the whole matter."[7]

Billy Graham: "Jesus called the devil 'the father of lies' (John 8:44). Does this mean the devil is directly responsible for every doubt we have? Not necessarily; often doubts come from within our own hearts and minds. But in reality it doesn't matter where our doubts come from; the important thing is what we do with them."[8]

The Bible also depicts many characters who were barraged by doubt. We will explore several of those more closely as the book unfolds. But for the moment, think about Sarah when she laughed at the thought of being pregnant in her nineties.[9] Can you blame her? We would all agree she had good reason to doubt. This same doubt splinter was in the mind of Habakkuk as he wrestled with God's justice, asking, "Why do you idly look at wrong?"[10]

The barb was in Zechariah's brain when he was told his wife

would bear him a son in old age.[11] Like father, like son, the splinter was also in the mind of Zechariah's son, John the Baptist. In fact, it got so bad for John that he wondered if Jesus was even the Messiah.[12] The shock of John's doubt is accentuated by the role he served as the confident forerunner and proclaimer that Jesus was indeed the Messiah.

The splinter was in Thomas's mind when he said, "Unless I see in his hands the mark of the nails, and place my finger into the mark of the nails, and place my hand into his side, I will never believe."[13] Ouch. No wonder we refer to him as Doubting Thomas. Thomas needed to see the resurrected Christ in order to believe, but for others, even seeing wasn't enough. After Jesus's resurrection He appeared to His disciples, and "when they saw him they worshiped him, but *some doubted*."[14]

....
The Bible is a book full of doubters.
....

Amazing, right? But do you get the picture here? The Bible is a book full of doubters. And guess what they all have in common?

They were all *believers.*

Splintered believers.

Doubting believers.

Torn believers.

Humans. Like you and me.

Sounds like an oxymoron, doesn't it? But all of these believers eventually learned to *doubt toward faith.*

And if this isn't shocking enough, consider Jesus. Yes, the Savior of the world, offering up a heartrending *why* from the cross. He not only had splinters in His flesh as His opened wounds rubbed against a coarse, wooden beam, but He also had a splinter in His mind. It showed up while He hung there, sinlessly crying out in His human-ity, "My God, my God, why have you forsaken me?"[15] Is that not the horror of all doubts?

Feeling forsaken is bad enough. But Jesus was feeling *God* forsaken.

Abandoned.

Forgotten.

Shunned.

Alone.

Left to Himself.

This is the misery we call doubt. But doubt doesn't belong exclu-sively to Bible characters or to theologians of our past. No, doubt is still here. Right now. Within you and within me. It is ever pervasive. It's still robbing Christians of their joy, rendering them powerless and hopeless. It is no respecter of persons, giving no regard to one's age, race, gender, or occupation. Like a virus, it attacks. It seeks to dissolve our faith and just might succeed...if we let it.

In their book *Philosophy of Religion*, C. Stephen Evans and R. Zachary Manis remind us that "the great saints are...not people who were always free of doubt, but rather people who were able to deal with their doubts and act decisively in spite of them"[16] That's what these characters learned. To proceed *faith-ward* even in the face of their doubts. That's not easy to do. But it can be done.

An Inner Anguish

Doubt often leaves its victims in a state of desperation. There is an inner anguish associated with doubt. Like a lingering headache, it pounds with every beat of our heart, enslaving us with inner tur-moil. Doubt can leave us emotionally wasted.

Lonely.

Confused.

Depressed.

Feeling hopeless.

Wanting to give up.

It can even lead once sold-out believers to contemplate suicide as they abandon all hope and embrace nihilism.[17] Doubt's lingering effects drain and deplete our intimacy with Jesus, making us feel fake around more confident believers. At times we even feel hypocritical as we doubt in the dark, away from possible ridicule or condemnation. Doubt can suffocate us. That's why the church must respond. And fast.

....

> Doubt's lingering effects deplete our
> intimacy with Jesus, making us feel fake
> around more confident believers.

....

Gone are the days (if they ever existed) of the American Christian utopia. This is not your father's "Christian America." And on top of all this, our nation's youth are leaving the church at record rates, and feeding this departure is a plethora of unchecked doubts.

I have the privilege of hosting an internationally recognized YouTube program called *The One Minute Apologist*.[18] On our program, I seek to provide biblical answers to questions puzzling both believers and nonbelievers alike. Our motto is "providing credible answers to curious questions," and I often interview scholars to get their professional perspective. As a result, I receive emails and questions from all over the world. Sometimes people, such as this teenage girl, are desperate for answers to their doubts:

Hello, my name is "Jan." I'm a seventeen-year-old Christian. I've been a Christian for many, many years. I've always had God inside of me keeping me comforted, but lately I've been in what I call a "crisis of belief." I've been having doubts in my head about the Bible and what it says.

For example: How's it physically possible for one to rise from the dead? Why isn't God there to help me when I really need Him? Doesn't the Bible say that He will help?

Sometimes the doubts are statements that electrocute my mind and belief, such as "You're wasting your time." Or "You're believing a fantasy" and "It's only a part of your brain that makes you believe."

But it's not like I want to believe these doubts. Because when I think of them, something burns in my heart and mind. My depression begins to act up really badly. Lately, I've had many anxiety attacks about it along with other stress. It's not helpful when atheists surround me in my school too. There really aren't many people I can ask for help. So I'm asking you. What do I do? Because I'm scared to say *I'm lost*.

Can you sense her agony?

Her emptiness?

Her confusion?

Have you ever had those thoughts or felt like Jan? Perhaps her agony is *your* agony. Oh, how I wish I could remove the splinter from Jan's mind...and yours.

My Own Journey

I too am a man of doubt. At times during my faith journey I have felt like I was hanging off the edge of a cliff by my fingernails.

I have known the inner anguish and despair caused by doubt. I've experienced the agony of wondering if my faith is even for real, even as a pastor and yes, even as an apologist. Perhaps you're asking yourself, "How can a Christian pastor who publicly defends the faith possibly struggle with doubt? Aren't pastors and apologists supposed to be beyond all that?"

> At times during my faith journey I have felt like I was hanging off the edge of a cliff by my fingernails.

Believe it or not, these people may struggle more than non-pastors and non-apologists because their full-time job is to wrestle with the most difficult questions posed against Christianity. Andrew Hoffecker, professor of church history at Gordon-Conwell, put it like this, "Apologists are no different from others who live under effects from the Fall. Athletes choke, writers suffer from blocks, and apologists doubt."[19]

I believe this is the point where every apologist and pastor responds with a heartfelt "Amen." Make no mistake about it, there's a cost to defending the Christian faith. You cannot give a rational answer for Christianity without facing the hardest questions raised against it. To ignore the questions is to remain naïve and useless in any attempt to help fellow doubters. As a Christian, it's my responsibility to contend for the faith, and as rewarding as this can be, it's definitely not without a cost.

My faith journey started off so simple. I was in search of answers to two questions: *What's my purpose in life?* and *How do I get rid of my guilt?* Christianity provided answers to my burning questions, especially with my deep sense of guilt before God. In the gospel, I found not only a remedy to relieve my guilt, but also meaning for my life through Jesus Christ.

When I look back to the early stages of my faith, I was ignorant of many things. For example, I didn't realize the church was fractured into over forty thousand denominations, many with competing views. Nor did I realize that for nearly every Christian doctrine I would learn, there were *at least* three ways to view or interpret that doctrine. Will Jesus return *before* the tribulation (pre-tribulation), in the *middle* of it (mid-tribulation), or at the *end* of it (post-tribulation)? Did God create the universe in six days (young earth theory), in stages (progressive creationism), or over thousands of years (day-age theory)? Did Jesus die on the cross to pay a ransom on our behalf (ransom theory), to become our substitute (substitutionary theory), or to fulfill the moral law (moral-influence theory)? Or is it a combination of all the above (combinational theory)?

These are important issues to many people. And though some of our theological disagreements have no bearing on salvation, they are nevertheless still there. Christianity isn't some slick little package that fits easily together. No.

It's messy.

Mind-racking.

Even exhausting at times.

....

> I'd be lying if I said there aren't moments
> that I miss the days when I didn't even
> know what questions to ask.

....

Ours is not a faith without questions. And as a new believer I was ignorant of so many of them. I had no idea there were so many difficulties, questions, objections, and so much vitriol toward the Christian faith. But this became clearer to me over time. And I'd be lying if I said there aren't moments that I miss the days when I didn't even know what questions to ask. Or what doubts to doubt. As the saying goes, "Ignorance is bliss." Ignorance may be bliss, but it's not reality. Besides, many of my doubts have actually led me to the truth as I relentlessly pursued answers to my difficult questions of faith.

However, the more I learn, the more I'm faced with my own finitude. I'll never have all the answers to all my questions, at least this side of heaven. I could list the hundreds of questions that I have found solid answers to. I could also list the numerous questions that still puzzle and confuse me. Nevertheless, I love the God I doubt. And besides, it's not like doubt is exclusively a Christian experience. As we'll see, doubt touches every faith and belief system. *Doubt is not merely a Christian problem, it's a human problem.* It affects us all. The question is, which faith can support itself with substantive evidence? Which faith earns the right to have people place their trust in it?

....

I'll never have all the answers to all my
questions, at least this side of heaven.

....

Concerning my personal doubts, two things really work against me. First, I'm an analyzer. Second, I tend to obsess. When you put those two qualities together, you end up with an obsessive-analyzer. That sounds a bit scary, doesn't it? It means I can tweak a little too much over unanswered questions.

Some people obsess but rarely analyze. Others analyze but they don't obsess. It's my opinion that those most susceptible to doubt struggle with both of these. Like a double-shot of espresso, we get twice as much energy (and sometimes *nervous* energy) from our doubts.

This obsessive-analyzer personality often demands absolute certainty when searching for answers. But this demand is too high. It's not attainable. It's out of our reach. In our finitude we have to be okay with unanswered questions. We have to resign ourselves to live with some mystery. Even some tension.

This stuff we call Christianity can be confusing at times. I once heard philosopher Peter Kreeft say, "If you're never confused, you're either God or an animal, but you're not a philosopher." So we continue to ask our questions. We philosophize. We use rationale and reason. We think and ponder. We seek and search and dig. And we remember all along, with thankfulness, that ours is a reasonable faith, though still a *faith*. We heed the biblical challenge that says, "the just shall live *by his faith*."[20]

There's no need for faith if we have all the answers. But having *all* the answers means we're God, and that's impossible—there's only one God, only one "Know-It-All." And the quicker we realize that, the better off we will be. And the smaller the chances are that the stress of doubt will conquer our mind and emotions.

··

There's no need for faith if we have all the answers.

··

Dissolving Doubt

I wish I could give you a money-back guarantee that after reading this book you'll be able to kiss doubt goodbye, forever. Or that you can once and for all time shout to your doubts, "Hasta la vista, baby!" But I'm afraid it's not quite that easy. At least for most people it isn't. While some may indeed find freedom forever from their doubts, most believers will discover a healthy *approach* to dealing with doubts. A way to manage them, to live with them, and in some cases, to silence certain doubts altogether.

I can tell you with confidence, though, that through the principles you'll discover in this book, you can learn how to process your doubts and, by God's grace, be able to live without that nagging headache each day. Though occasionally doubt may creep up on you and even temporarily incapacitate your spiritual life, it won't have to last forever because of the skills we'll discuss together here. That is something to hope for.

As I've reflected on Mother Teresa's four-decade battle with doubt, I can only wonder if she could have removed the splinter many years earlier, or perhaps lessened its size, had she been more open about her doubts. Maybe she was afraid to confess this weakness, as admission often comes at the cost of ridicule and people losing confidence in you. However, there shouldn't be a cost for the person who simply and sincerely has legitimate questions to explore. Rather, the church should welcome this "doubt dialogue" by gently guiding Jesus's bride to doubt toward faith.

Thankfully, Archbishop Perier provided some much-needed hope in his reply to Mother Teresa's angst. I hope his words lead you to hope as well:

> With regard to the feeling of loneliness, of abandonment, of not being wanted, of darkness of the soul, it is a state well known by spiritual writers and directors of conscience. This is willed by God in order to attach us to Him alone, an antidote to our external activities, and also, like temptation, a way of keeping us humble in the midst of applauses, publicity, praises, appreciation, etc. and success. To feel that we are nothing, that we can do nothing is the realization of a fact.[21]

We are far from being betrayed or abandoned; God has not left us alone. Granted, at times He may appear detached and even distant. But in those moments we must remember *it's a test*, not a cruel, random, pointless punishment.

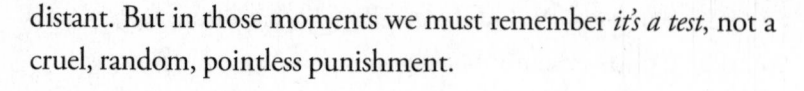

> We are far from being betrayed or
> abandoned; God has not left us alone.

But a test with *purpose*. A test designed to deepen our faith, not erase it. This test will help us declare our faith, not deny it. Doubts often dissolve when we wholly attach ourselves to God by clinging to faith in the midst of our inner darkness.

God isn't looking for another Mother Teresa. He's just looking for honest believers who are willing to walk through the dark tunnels of doubt...all the while holding the unseen Hand of assurance, hope, and peace.

Doubt Reflections

- *Doubt is not a Christian problem. It's a* human *problem.*

- *A lack of doubt doesn't necessarily mean you're super-spiritual. It may mean you're shallow.*

- *Doubt must be addressed lest your doubts erode your faith.*

Questions for Further Thought and Discussion

1. Bobby writes, "Doubt is no respecter of persons. Seasoned saint or hardened sinner, we're all susceptible." Why is this so?

2. Have the myriad theological positions out there ever made your faith feel complicated, perhaps even causing you to miss the simplicity of the earliest stages of your Christian walk?

3. Do you find it comforting to know you're not alone in your doubts, that you're preceded by a long tradition of doubters both in the Bible and throughout church history?

4. What types of questions create the most doubt for you? And how have you sought to keep your faith alive with the tension of unanswered or unsatisfactorily answered questions?

5. Watch this interview I did with apologist Os Guinness on *The One Minute Apologist* (www.youtube.com/watch?v=gY0DXkXhUE4) and answer the following question: Which direction do my doubts tend to go: toward faith or toward unbelief?

6. Would you be willing to pray for your pastors and apologists or Christian educators you know and ask God to grow them through their doubts and to protect them in the midst of doubt when it comes their way? I know they would appreciate it.

Chapter 3

JESUS CAN HANDLE YOUR DOUBTS

*"God appears far less threatened by
doubt than does his church."*

PHILIP YANCEY

*"Christ never failed to distinguish between doubt
and unbelief. Doubt is can't believe; unbelief is
won't believe. Doubt is honest; unbelief is obstinacy.
Doubt is looking for light; unbelief is content with
darkness. Loving darkness rather than light—that is
what Christ attacked and attacked unsparingly."*

HENRY DRUMMOND

Steve Jobs, the visionary and cofounder of Apple Inc., was one of the greatest entrepreneurs of all time. His technological ideas changed the world forever. In his highly acclaimed biography, *Steve Jobs,* Walter Isaacson pulls the skeleton of doubt out of Jobs's closet, demonstrating how haunting doubts contributed to his departure from Christianity. During his childhood years, Jobs attended a Lutheran church most Sundays, but this all changed when he turned thirteen. Isaacson portrays it as follows:

In July 1968 *Life* magazine published a shocking cover showing a pair of starving children in Biafra. Jobs took it to Sunday school and confronted the church's pastor. "If I raise my finger, will God know which one I'm going to raise even before I do it?"

The pastor answered, "Yes, God knows everything."

Jobs then pulled out the *Life* cover and asked, "Well, does God know about this and what's going to happen to those children?"

"Steve, I know you don't understand, but yes, God knows about that."[1]

And that was it.

No answer.

No apologetic.

No sympathy.

No reasoning.

No "Let's talk about this, young man."

Just a simple, "Yes, Steve, God knows about that."

After that conversation Jobs left the church...*never to return*. A trite answer shifted his wonder and doubt to unbelief. Just like that. From that point forward, Steve Jobs was finished with the God of Christianity. He later become a Zen Buddhist and remained one until the day he died. Tragic.

A Place for Doubters

So what happened that day in Jobs's church? Simply put, the pastor couldn't handle young Steve's doubts. He either didn't want to or know how to. The result either way is still heart wrenching. Sadly, that is par for the course in many churches today. Many doubters struggle, fearing if they expose their doubts they'll be treated as pariahs or outcasts or heretics.

> Many doubters struggle, fearing if they
> expose their doubts they'll be treated
> as pariahs or outcasts or heretics.

Kara Powell, coauthor of *Sticky Faith* and the executive director of the Fuller Youth Institute, shares some alarming discoveries. After tracking five hundred youth-group graduates three years into their college experience, she writes, "In our *Sticky Faith* research, geared to help young people develop a Christian faith that lasts, a common narrative emerged: When young people asked tough questions about God at church, often during elementary or middle school, they were told by well-meaning church leaders and teachers, 'We don't ask those sorts of questions about God here.'"[2]

It's lamentable that many churches today are threatened by tough questions. They aren't prepared to handle people's doubts and therefore ignore them, condemn them, or flippantly dismiss them. To communicate that asking questions is wrong *is wrong*. If Christianity really contains the truth, then it can certainly handle life's most-challenging questions. Can it not? Unfortunately, unprepared or uncaring Christians often aren't ready to help people like Steve Jobs and countless others to deal with their doubts. And so many doubters drift out to sea, believing there is no safe place for them to process their doubts. They become spiritual castaways.

*If Christianity really contains the truth,
then it can certainly handle life's most-
challenging questions. Can it not?*

Perhaps you've been doing a little drifting yourself. Have you been taught that you're not allowed to doubt? Not allowed to ask the hard and sticky questions about God? Ever felt awkward because you're too inquisitive? If so, you're not alone. This is the sad reality for many doubters. Philip Yancey, a well-known Christian author, was no stranger to doubt. He openly shares his own experience of growing up in a church where doubts weren't welcome:

> As a child I attended a church that had little room for inquisitiveness. If you doubted or questioned, you sinned. I learned to conform, as you must in a church like that. Meanwhile those deep doubts, those deep questions, didn't get answered in a satisfactory way. The danger of such a church like that—and there are many— is that by saying, "Don't doubt, just believe," you don't really resolve the doubts. They tend to resurface in a more toxic form. [3]

Ever had to learn to conform and not ask the hard questions? Ever been left alone to wrestle in silence with your doubts?

Have your questions been silenced? Ignored? Minimized? Mocked?

If so, I've got good news for you. Perhaps your pastor, church, friends, or family can't handle your doubts. But here's something you may not know.

Jesus *can* handle your doubts.

Yes, Jesus. The long-awaited Messiah and creator of the universe.

That Jesus. And He not only can handle your doubts—apparently He also welcomes them.

An Unsuspecting Doubter

Nowhere is this better portrayed than in Jesus's interactions with John the Baptist. John was an odd figure to say the least. Aside from maintaining a diet of locusts and wild honey, he also struggled with fashion issues, sporting a garment of camel hair, a leather belt, and a pair of sandals. Not a candidate for *GQ* magazine. Imagine a guest looking like that showing up at your church one Sunday morning. I mean this guy was way out there. Truth be told, if he were alive today, he'd have a hard time landing a job in any American pulpit. Can you see the Twitter feed, "#whatswiththeguyinthecamelhairapparel?"

Yet, this man was 100 percent sold out for Christ. You wouldn't know it by looking at him, but John was all about one thing—preparing the way for Jesus. Making Him known. In fact, his life motto was "More of Jesus, less of me."[4]

From the wilderness of Judea he beckoned people, crying out, "Repent, for the kingdom of heaven is at hand."[5] And like a great evangelist pointing people to Jesus, he declared, "Behold, the Lamb of God, who takes away the sin of the world!"[6] But make no mistake, in spite of his oddities, his resume was golden. Here's the short list:

Positive Traits

- set apart from birth
- son of a priest
- cousin of Jesus
- a God-called prophet

- Jesus's forerunner

- an unashamed preacher

- a disciplemaker

- led many to repentance

- and he even baptized the Messiah

Can you say, "Impressive"?

But as stunning as this list may be, John still had what some may say was a flaw in his faith, a crack in his character. You see, John was also a *doubter*.

Wait. What? Are you serious? You mean to tell me John the Baptist had a bout with doubt?

....

Are you serious? John the Baptist
had a bout with doubt?

....

Absolutely. That's because it's easy to be bold and confident when you're free. But wait until your head is about to go to the chopping block and see what happens. In that moment, any sane person wants to be sure their beliefs are on target. Any person about to step into eternity ought to do some serious soul-searching. And John is no exception. Having been imprisoned for challenging Herod's unlawful marriage, John knew his time was short. As the hourglass was running empty, John slipped into a state of panic spelled D-O-U-B-T.

Seeds of Doubt

This begs the question, "How does a man so confident about Christ all his life become so overwhelmed by doubt right before his death?" John's got to be one of the last guys in the Bible I'd picture struggling with doubt. But he did. And while Scripture doesn't tell us *why* he doubted, here are a few possibilities that may have provoked his doubt.

Perhaps he thought, *Jesus, if You really are the Messiah, then why am I still stuck in this dungeon?* It might also be that John was confused by the nature of Jesus's kingship. Instead of overthrowing the Roman kingdom and setting up His own, Jesus seemed to have a different kingdom agenda. John may have thought, *Is this really the kingdom at hand we've all been waiting for and that I've been preaching about? If so, why am I in chains?* Blown expectations are often the source of our doubt too. We expect God to operate a certain way, and when He doesn't, doubt begins to reverberate within us.

> We expect God to operate a certain way, and when He doesn't, doubt begins to reverberate within us.

I think it's equally probable that John's doubt was triggered by *fear.* Think about it. Here's a guy who was imprisoned by Herod Antipas himself. And if you know anything about Herod, you know he's not the kind of guy you reason with over a caramel macchiato at Starbucks. Herod was a morally weak leader. His father (Herod the Great) was the one who issued orders to slaughter all the male babies two years old and under around the time of Jesus's birth.[7] Like his father, Herod Antipas had no fear of God. John knew the minute that he was arrested, he was a dead man walking. He knew his future was, shall we say, grim. And there's nothing like the thought of imminent death to bring us face-to-face with what really matters—our beliefs. Perhaps John thought to himself, *Alright, it was one thing to confidently preach out in the wilderness as a free man, but if I'm going to die as a prisoner, I really want to be sure that Jesus is the real deal.*

So what does he do? Thankfully, the Bible tells us. In Matthew 11, we see the story of John's doubt unfold: "Now when John heard in prison about the deeds of the Christ, he sent word by his disciples and said to him, 'Are you the one who is to come, or shall we look for another?'"[8]

Can you detect the doubt?

The uncertainty?

The confusion?

"Is Jesus legit, or did I just waste thirty years of my life living a fairy tale? I have to know."

Maybe you're thinking to yourself, *What happened to John's unflappable conviction? Where's his confident assertion that Jesus is the Messiah?* Earlier he was shamelessly stating, "Behold, the Lamb of God, who takes away the sin of the world," and now he's shaking in his sandals, wondering, "Could I have missed it?"

One moment you believe beyond all doubt, and
the next moment you can't get beyond your doubt.

Can you relate? One moment your faith is sizzling and the next it's fizzling. One moment you believe beyond all doubt, and the next moment you can't get beyond your doubt. One moment you're assertively declaring your faith, and the next moment you're ashamedly doubting it.

How does this happen? It's called *being human*. And this shared trait makes everyone of us susceptible to doubt. Including John.

And there is nothing like a little fear to call your faith into question. To create panic. Or squeamishness. Or uncertainty. And when your fear turns to doubt, one thing every doubting believer longs for is a heavy dose of Christian assurance. You know, some good old-fashioned comfort. And that's exactly what John's about to get from Jesus. Let's keep reading:

> And Jesus answered them, "Go and tell John what you hear and see: the blind receive their sight and the lame walk, lepers are cleansed and the deaf hear, and the dead are raised up, and the poor have good news preached to them. And blessed is the one who is not offended by me."[9]

As a student of the Old Testament, John would have known that those prophesied miraculous signs would be true only of the Messiah.[10] Can you hear the sigh of relief from John's disciples? Phew. And off they went to John with some freshly packed assurance. Then Jesus said to the remaining crowd as they departed:

> "What did you go out into the wilderness to see? A reed shaken by the wind? What then did you go out to see? A man dressed in soft clothing? Behold, those who wear soft clothing are in kings' houses. What then did you go out to see? A prophet? Yes, I tell you, and more than a prophet. This is he of whom it is written,

> 'Behold, I send my messenger before your face, who will prepare your way before you.'

> Truly, I say to you, among those born of women there has arisen no one greater than John the Baptist."[11]

Incredible. No doubt Jesus's words gave John assurance, comfort, and *relief.*

Every sincere believer should be penetrated to the core with encouragement from these words. Not only did Jesus offer John solid assurance, but He also offered up a twofold blessing of *assurance* and *affirmation*. This is the place where we all pick up our jaws. Christ's words here are nothing short of spectacular. His message for John wasn't, "I know you don't understand, John, but just believe." Or, "We don't ask questions like that around here, John. You should know that." Nope. Instead, He comforted John with *evidence*. And if that wasn't enough, far from being disappointed with John, Jesus even dished out the greatest compliment of his earthly ministry, "No one greater has been born of a woman."

Wow. All that on the heels of *doubt*.

Perhaps selfishly, I'm glad guys like John battled with doubt. I'm thankful I can learn from men like him who've wrestled through their doubts, and I'd like to unpack a few nuggets I've gathered from John's encounter.

First, be vulnerable enough to reveal your doubts to others.

Think about how difficult it had to be for John to share his doubts with his followers. It's one thing for a Christian to doubt and another for a Christian *leader* to doubt. Few things are worse than hanging around a super pious person who thinks they've got life all figured out. That's not John. He was authentic to the core. To the *end*. And that authenticity caused him to be a very vulnerable man.

> Think about how difficult it had to be for John
> to share his doubts with his followers.

Consider this: John sent his disciples to Jesus *with his doubts*. That's what you call an entrusting leader. It takes a lot for a guy with John's stature to be real. A lot is on the line here.

Try standing in his disciples' sandals for a moment. You've been following John for a while and he's been telling you a thousand times, "Jesus is the Messiah." And now he's asking you to go find out if He really is? Can you see their blank stares? Can you sense their confusion? Perhaps even their frustration? We can only speculate what was going on in their minds, but I can just picture their reaction: "Um, excuse me, Mr. John, but I thought you already told us Jesus *is* the Messiah. The *One*. The *Only*. And now you're doubting? Is this some kind of a joke?"

Talk about a gutsy move on John's part. He went all out when he revealed his doubts. But what's the alternative? Stuffing your doubts? I wonder where that would've gotten him. Dying with doubt leads to a fear-filled ending in this life. No, John knew that he needed to get real to get the confidence he needed. He needed to double-check his faith foundation to make sure it was rock solid. And it was.

> Do you have an inner circle of trusted
> friends you can reveal your doubts to?

How about you? Do you have an inner circle of trusted friends you can reveal your doubts to? Some close buddies or girlfriends you can be real with? A church that isn't threatened by your questions? A mom or dad who would welcome a hearing? And if so, are you willing to be vulnerable enough to reveal them? To say, "Hey guys, I could really use some help here. I'm struggling. Can I borrow your ear?" I challenge you to give it a shot.

Second, get in the habit of taking your doubts to Jesus.

John exemplified this by directing his disciples to the right source. He sent them directly to Jesus. He didn't beat around the bush.

As Christians, we too have direct access to Jesus. You may be thinking, *There's a big difference between John and me. Did you forget that Jesus was walking the earth when John was here? That He was approachable? I mean He was seen, touched, and could be heard. You get what I'm saying?*

And the good news is that Jesus is just as approachable to us as He was to John and his disciples. In fact, He's even *more* approachable. Remember, He's our great mediator in heaven who hears our prayers—even today. Even right now.[12] And at just the right time, He will respond with grace and mercy during our time of need and doubt.

Our job is to go to Him through prayer with our doubts. And prayer is simply conversing with God. As the great High Priest of heaven, Jesus hears your prayers. In fact, unlike John, who had to send his disciples to Jesus, we can go straight to Him in prayer. He's there for us, ready to listen. The question is, are you ready to speak?

Third, when you do take your doubts to Jesus, be specific.

That's exactly what John did. His question wasn't general or vague. Not at all. He knew what his doubt was and expressed it specifically. John wanted to know if Jesus was "the one who is to come." The Messiah.

....

Identify your doubts and then take
them to Jesus in prayer.

....

So here's my advice. Identify your doubts and then take them to Jesus in prayer. Go to Him and say, "Lord, I'm struggling with (<u>fill in the blank</u>).

Be real.

Be honest.

And be specific.

Don't hold back. Seriously, respectfully, lay it all before Him. Sadly, when people are taught that they can't doubt, they learn to fake it not only around other believers, but they also learn to fake it with God. Now *that's* a tragedy. When you exercise authenticity with God by praying specifically, it will not only be a relief to get those doubts off your chest, but it'll also help you to develop a deeper intimacy with Jesus. And there's nothing like renewed intimacy to quiet your doubts.

Unfortunately, many who are analytical are often resistant to prayer. They chase down all their questions through philosophy and apologetics and fail to chase God's heart in prayer. While reading is good and strongly suggested, you cannot forsake seeking Jesus *specifically* about your doubts. If you do, you'll be at risk of stuffing your head while emptying your heart. You'll wither while you wonder.

Granted, prayer is a bit mystical. I get it. But all I can say is there's an inner assurance available for the believer who truly seeks God in prayer. As God told Jeremiah, "You will seek me and find me, *when you seek me with all your heart.*"[13] So take your doubts to Jesus in prayer, and as you do, remember to exercise faith.

> There's an inner assurance available for the believer who truly seeks God in prayer.

Jesus's half brother James gave us some good advice when he

wrote, "If any of you lacks wisdom, let him ask God, who gives generously to all without reproach, and it will be given him. But let him ask in faith, with no doubting, for the one who doubts is like a wave of the sea that is driven and tossed by the wind."[14] He's spot on. Nothing will toss your emotions around more than doubts. What is James's invitation in prayer? To doubt toward faith *prayerfully.* He's saying, "You may doubt in everyday life, you may not be sure what to do, but when it comes to seeking God, it's time to put your faith on."

Ask. Receive. Believe.

Fourth, never forget that Jesus can handle your doubts.

I love how Jesus responded to John's desperate doubts. After hearing John's concern through his disciples about whether or not He really was the Messiah, Jesus doesn't express disappointment or irritation. Just how does He respond?

Was He shocked?

Did He panic?

Did He write John off?

Nope. Not one bit.

And why? Simply put: *Because Jesus can handle our doubts.* That's why. And that's a wonderful thought.

He can also discern whether our doubt comes from a sincere place or not. Whether we just feel like doubting for the sake of doubting or if we really desire to deal with our doubts. And there is a difference. A *big* one. As we just saw, Jesus knew that John needed a little assurance and that's exactly what He gave him. But not empty assurance. He assured John with the *evidence.* And that's key. My friend and fellow apologist J. Warner Wallace nicely put it:

When those times of doubt arise, it's important for us to return to the evidence that brought us here in the first place. That's what Jesus did for John; He provided clear evidence that helped John "connect the dots" and reminded John of Jesus' identity. Given all the other things that Jesus could have done or said, it's remarkable that Jesus used evidence to assuage John's doubt.[15]

Jesus was essentially saying to John, "Hey, you know all the things the Messiah was prophesied to do? Well, guess what? It's happening. I'm doing it. All of it. People are getting healed, the gospel is being preached, and lives are being changed. And oh, by the way, John, yes, I *AM* the Messiah. I *AM* the Man. In fact, *I'm more than a Man.*"

....

> Far from what you may have been taught,
> Jesus is not fuming at your doubts.

....

Isn't it refreshing to know that Jesus can handle your doubts? And what better person to entrust your doubts to? Far from what you may have been taught, Jesus is not fuming at your doubts. Seeing that He welcomes our doubts should increase our confidence to take them directly to Him whenever they arise.

Finally, take comfort in knowing that doubters are still valuable to Jesus.

It's easy to feel overwhelmed when you doubt. Doubts have a way of making our thoughts and emotions irrational, creating extra doses of life stress. But it's nice to know that Jesus can discern beneath our doubts. Even though John doubted Jesus, John was still valuable to Him.

As John's disciples left, Jesus had some final words about John. It's possible that the crowd thought, *This guy's not legit. He's a flip-flopper. He's a good for nothing. All talk, no action.* Jesus took a moment to openly affirm John. He basically said, "Hey, gang, John's not some prophet easily tossed by every new wind of doctrine. No, he's the real deal." Jesus says in affirming John that he's not "a reed shaken by the wind."[16] In other words, John isn't someone whose entire life is marked by doubt.

Jesus then says the unbelievable, "Truly, I say to you, among those born of women there has arisen *no one greater* than John the Baptist. Yet the one who is least in the kingdom of heaven is greater than he."[17]

Think about it. Right on the heels of his doubts, Jesus says, "No one has been born greater..." Gary Habermas writes: "We dare not call John the Baptist's doubt unbelief, or we would be contradicting our Lord's assertion that he was the most (godly) righteous man born of a woman."[18]

....

> Jesus affirms that doubting
> *toward faith* is a good thing.

....

It turns out that even the godliest among us can have fits of doubt. And this isn't Jesus affirming doubt as a good thing. It's not. It's Jesus affirming that doubting *toward faith* is a good thing. It's also His affirmation that John is still valuable, in spite of his doubt.

I don't know about you, but I'm thinking it's sure nice to know that Jesus loves and values doubters. Even more so, that He loves and values you and me.

Something Worth Pondering

After reflecting upon Steve Jobs's departure from the church, Kara Powell writes:

> I often wonder what would have happened if Steve Jobs's pastor had walked through his doubts with him. What would have happened if the pastor had answered, "Steve, that's a great question. I don't know the answer, but I'd love to meet again to study Scripture and see if we can figure it out together"? Is it possible that our world would be a better place if Jobs's entrepreneurial energy had been channeled not just toward technology but also gospel-minded purposes?[19]

I guess we'll never know, but it's sure worth pondering. The way I see it, the church can learn a lot from Jesus on dealing with troubled doubters. It really is sad to think about all the people who were taught growing up, "Don't ever question God." This false teaching has created many hopeless doubters. And many of them are closet doubters. They reason, "If I can't talk about my doubts at church and I can't talk to God about my doubts, then what am I to do?"

> The church can learn a lot from Jesus
> on dealing with troubled doubters.

Here's what you can do: *Go to Jesus.* It's that simple. The next time you're barraged doubting in the dark, take your doubts to Jesus.

He can handle them. And as long as you live, whenever you face a bout with doubt, remember Jesus's words to John the Baptist. Seek the evidence you need. And then hear Him affirm not only who He is, but also who you are to Him.

Doubt. Toward. Jesus.

Doubt Reflections

- *If Christianity really is the truth, then it can certainly handle life's largest and most-challenging questions.*

- *Your pastor, church, friends, or family may not be able to handle your doubts, but rest assured Jesus can.*

- *Nothing can quiet your doubts faster than a renewed intimacy with Jesus.*

Questions for Further Thought and Discussion

1. Did anything in particular stand out to you in this chapter?

2. Have you heard any stories similar to that of Steve Jobs? Or have you ever been treated similarly, perhaps with silence, rejection, or rebuke?

3. How did the church ever come to a place where it wouldn't help doubters process their doubts or even discuss them?

4. What can we learn from Jesus about processing doubts with others?

5. There's a difference between doubting for doubt's sake and doubting because you're genuinely seeking an answer. What do you think the difference is, and why is it important to not just doubt for the sake of doubt?

6. How can the church do a better job saying, "Not only can Jesus handle your doubts, but our church can too"? Obviously that doesn't mean we have all the answers to everybody's questions. But it does mean we are eager to help sincere and authentic doubters doubt toward faith.

Chapter 4

DOUBT TRIGGERS: PART 1

*"Skill in answering doubt depends largely
on skill in questioning doubt."*

Os Guinness

"Doubt is not a pleasant condition, but certainty is absurd."

Voltaire

Chances are the name Hermann Samuel Reimarus doesn't ring a bell. And it probably wouldn't unless you lived in Germany during the eighteenth century. Reimarus was a well-known German philosopher whose Christian faith was hijacked by a barrage of doubts. Eventually his doubts, which he quietly cataloged in writing, evolved into a four-thousand-page critique of the Bible called *Fragments*. Though he never formally published his work, Reimarus revealed his doubts to a few close friends and two of his children.

When his massive tome was published posthumously, it created quite the frenzy. Reimarus had sapped the Scriptures of all things supernatural, denying special revelation, miracles, the deity of Christ, and most importantly the resurrection of Christ. He concluded that Jesus was a deluded man with visions of messianic grandeur that were obviously never fulfilled. In the end, Christianity was nothing but a hoax. A fraud. A hopeless fiction.[1]

Reimarus's doubts triggered a domino effect
that rendered his Christian faith lifeless.

Reimarus is a classic picture of a so-called Christian doubting toward unbelief. His doubts triggered a domino effect that rendered his Christian faith lifeless. Thankfully, for every Reimarus there are other intellects who have been equally curious or intrigued by the same questions, but experienced a different outcome—a deeper faith and assurance of God's Word. Reimarus grew obsessively analytical as he was buffeted by doubts. As apologist Alister McGrath writes, "Doubt is like an attention-seeking child: when you pay attention to it, it demands that you pay even more attention. This is a vicious cycle that is difficult to escape from. If we feed our doubts, they'll grow."[2] McGrath is in no way suggesting some sort of intellectual suicide. Rather, he realizes there is a proper approach to dealing with doubt.[3]

Every doubter must ask, "What's
behind my doubts?"

Each of us must identify our doubt triggers without being crushed by them. We need to go beneath the surface and explore the triggers of our own doubt. This topic is so important that I've dedicated the next two chapters to explore these different doubt triggers. Even so, the list is far from exhaustive. Every doubter must ask,

"What's behind my doubts?" What's the source? The root? The trigger? Like every disease, doubt has an initial cause. Let's now explore the first three of these doubt triggers.

Trigger 1: The Apparent Ridiculous

As Christians, we sometimes chat about all the weird things others, such as Mormons, Wiccans, Hindus, or Jehovah's Witnesses, believe. But we Christians believe some pretty bizarre things too, do we not? I'm talking about those stories in the Bible that read straight up weird to the modern eye. And Scripture is replete with such head scratching stories as:

- Noah and the Great Flood[4]
- The parting of the Red Sea[5]
- Manna raining from heaven[6]
- The fall of Jericho[7]
- Shadrach, Meshach, and Abednego in the fiery furnace without even one thread of their clothing being singed[8]
- Or how about Daniel in the lions' den[9]
- Or Balaam and his talking donkey[10] (Can you say, "Bizarre"?)
- Or Ezekiel lying on his left side for 390 days to depict Israel's judgment, only to change sides and lie on his right side for another 40 days to depict Judah's judgment[11] (Chiropractor anyone?)
- What about Samson singlehandedly striking down a thousand Philistines with a donkey's jawbone,[12] or David taking out Goliath the giant,[13] or Jonah being

swallowed by an enormous fish,[14] or even the tongues of fire falling from the sky on Pentecost?[15]

These all illustrate a ubiquitous theme of the apparent ridiculous found in Scripture. And we're just scratching the surface. Seriously.

Perhaps this theme of the ridiculous is captured best after Sarah gives birth to Isaac at the ripe old age of ninety. (Yes, you read that correctly.) And Sarah was aware of the absurdity herself, stating, "God has made laughter for me; everyone who hears will laugh over me."[16] That is, they will laugh with amazement.

And yet, though bizarre, these stories are not without explanation. Through archaeological discoveries as in the case of Jericho, or the multiple attestations of flood stories in ancient history, or God doing something unique for His own sovereign purposes, there are solid, satisfactory answers to help you doubt toward faith. Nevertheless, the cover of your Bible could easily include a disclaimer that reads "Some Faith Required."

These biblical narratives sound so bizarre to the twenty-first-century reader that we must be careful not to read them through the lens of our contemporary culture. We have to grasp them in their own context because that's where God met the people involved. And it's also how He meets us—in our time. On our turf. In our *context*. Without this understanding we'll inevitably open the doors of doubt.[17]

I once heard that Larry King, the longtime host of *Larry King Live*, refused to believe in the Bible because he couldn't stomach the staggering passage where God commands Abraham to sacrifice his son Isaac.[18] According to King, only a barbaric God would dish out such a decree. And can you blame him? What would you think if someone told you to sacrifice your son or daughter? So how can we possibly imagine loving a God who could issue such a command?

We've got to step into the ancient
milieu and understand Scripture in
the context it was written in.

Remember what I just said? We can't impose a twenty-first-century worldview on an ancient context. We've got to step into the ancient milieu and understand Scripture in the context it was written in. With that in mind, is there an explanation that could assuage King's disbelief? Or even yours? If Larry King could hold his judgment for a moment and mentally travel back in time to consider the wider context, he could better digest what God was doing through Abraham in this *apparently ridiculous* story.

Abraham was called out of southern Mesopotamia, from Ur of the Chaldeans. He would've been keenly familiar with child sacrifice as the quintessential way to demonstrate one's faith. Furthermore, after departing Ur, he would've continued to hear about child sacrifice in ancient Canaan. Of course, this doesn't legitimize child sacrifice. Far from it. It just helps us see through the lens of Abraham for a moment.

With this in mind, we should ask, "Is it possible that Abraham saw this as an opportunity to demonstrate his absolute faith in God?" By grafting some New Testament insight into this discussion, we quickly become privy to the fact that Abraham believed that God could *literally* raise Isaac from the dead *even if he did sacrifice him.* Remember, Abraham believed that Isaac was the child God had promised to give him and Sarah. In the past, Abraham doubted toward *un*belief, anxiously taking Hagar (a servant girl) as a backup plan to produce the promised child. But now, lesson learned, he doubts toward *faith*, believing God's command is merely a test. The author of Hebrews scripted it like this:

> By faith Abraham, when he was tested, offered up Isaac, and he who had received the promises was in the act of offering up his only son, of whom it was said, "Through Isaac shall your offspring be named." He considered that God was able even to raise him from the dead, from which, figuratively speaking, he did receive him back.[19]

So now let's make sense of the apparent nonsense. From Abraham's vantage point, the command to sacrifice Isaac wasn't dished out by a cruel God after all. God was using an ancient belief to teach Abraham an important lesson about faith. As God, He wanted Abraham to know that He doesn't operate like the other so-called gods. And He doesn't expect His followers to sacrifice their children to Him either. This test was an opportunity for God to distinguish Himself from the erroneous beliefs of the surrounding culture of Abraham's time who horrifically practiced such atrocities. And besides, as the author of Hebrews states, it was a figurative test pointing to the ultimate sacrifice in Jesus Christ. God said, "I'll provide the sacrifice."

After a little analysis, it turns out that God agrees with Larry King on this one. He too has a holy disdain for child sacrifice. In time, not only would the Mosaic Law condemn child sacrifice, God actually would judge the Canaanites for such barbarism.

Can you now see how important it is for us to understand the context before quickly dismissing some of these seemingly bizarre Bible stories? I think Abraham would say to the critics, "Hey, step into my sandals and realize what may seem absurd to you actually made sense to us during our time."

Now, while this may help make sense of apparent nonsense, it is true that sometimes God asks us to do things that seem absurd, and a cultural explanation may not suffice. For example, while we can offer a contextual explanation for child sacrifice in Abraham's story, we cannot explain, through context, the miracle of Sarah giving birth to Isaac at age ninety. We just have to trust that God is the giver of life, and He can work through someone's reproductive system regardless of age. While it may seem ridiculous, it certainly isn't out of the realm of possibility for an all-powerful God.

> What at first glance seems ridiculous
> often turns out to not only grow our faith,
> but also to demonstrate how God really
> does uniquely work through us.

This idea of the apparent ridiculous is a subtheme running throughout Scripture, as God repeatedly asks His people to follow Him into the absurd. What at first glance seems ridiculous often turns out to not only grow our faith, but also to demonstrate how God really does uniquely work through us.

Trigger 2: Demanding Certainty

Another doubt trigger occurs when we demand absolute, 100 percent certainty regarding all matters of faith. Understand that this book would do you a great disservice if I left you with the impression that Christianity is supposed to answer *every* intellectual obstacle we encounter.

It doesn't. And it's not meant to. Think about it. If absolute certainty were the prerequisite for belief, you would never believe anything. Before belief would be possible, you'd have to complete an exhaustive, airtight study that demonstrated the truth of Christianity beyond a shadow of a doubt.

But who could do that? No one. You'd have to be...well, *God.*

We'd all have to hold off believing until we completed and confirmed a comprehensive case for Christianity. And that would take a lifetime...at least. Such a task is not only unreasonable for finite beings, it's also *impossible*. And if you could achieve certitude this side of heaven, faith would be unnecessary. Faith is the finite mind's best friend.

> If you could achieve certitude this side of heaven, faith would be unnecessary.

Here's a thought to digest: *In the absence of certainty, there's always room for doubt.* And this applies not only to the Christian but to everyone.

No one, in any belief system, can prove his or her faith with 100 percent certainty. But 100 percent certainty is also not required in order to believe in something or to have reasonable assurance that what you believe is true and trustworthy.

- I believe my wife when she says she'll be faithful to only me.
- I believe my friends when they say, "I'm telling you the truth."
- I believe the red light will turn green in a reasonable amount of time.
- I believe my government won't collapse tomorrow.
- I believe it will get dark tonight. I'm betting you believe that too.

None of the above examples is 100 percent guaranteed as there are potential scenarios that may prevent them from happening. And yet, I proceed by faith every day believing in all of them. Absolute certainty is not required for me to accept them. But some level of faith *is*.

So don't let others impale your faith on this issue when you can equally turn the tables on them. Nobody has 100 percent, absolute certainty. Not the scientist or the Muslim or the avid Scientologist. No one.

Alister McGrath writes,

> There will always be an element of doubt in any statement that goes beyond the world of logic and self-evident propositions. Christianity is not unique in this respect: an atheist or Marxist is confronted with the same dilemma. Anyone who wants to talk about the meaning of life has to make statements that rest on faith, not absolute certainty. Anyway, God isn't a proposition—he's a person. [20]

Nicely said, Alister.

Feeling certain and being certain

"But Bobby, I feel 100 percent certain that Christianity is true," you may contest. And I would add, we cannot confuse *feeling* certain and *being* certain. There's a difference. Mormons also feel certain their beliefs are true, as do Muslims, atheists, and many others. Feeling certain and being certain aren't necessarily equivalent.

....

We cannot confuse *feeling* certain and
being certain. There's a difference.

....

As we all know, feelings are fickle. One day your moods may sing the praises of your faith and the next day your moods will betray you, drowning you in the despair of doubt. Many people who walk around saying "I know with 100 percent certainty that my faith is true" haven't thought much about their faith. They're often blissfully naïve, which insulates them from an onslaught of doubts. But begin poking holes into their superficial claims of certainty, and they'll soon be gazing into the face of their own finitude.

The reality is, even those who *feel* 100 percent certain can't prove Christianity with 100 percent certainty. And we do the church a great disservice when we act like we can. Not to mention, we also set new believers up for a future doubt crisis when they realize things in our faith aren't as tidy as they once thought. In any event, we must avoid two extremes, this time as it relates to certainty. On one extreme we have philosophers like René Descartes who seek certainty through doubting everything, and on the other extreme are those who doubt nothing in order to feel good about their *supposed* certainty. Neither solution is helpful.

Philosopher J.P. Moreland writes,

> If you believe something, that does not mean you are *certain* that it is true. Rather, it means that you are at least more than 50 percent convinced the belief is true…The more certain you are of a belief, the more it becomes part of your very soul, and the more you rely on it as a basis for action.[21]

A friend of mine, who also happens to be a well-known Christian scholar, once said, "I'm about 80 percent sure that Christianity is true." I thought to myself, *Boy, that's not very encouraging.* He was essentially saying, "I have my doubts. I can't be 100 percent, but in the meantime, I doubt toward faith." And here's what I know about my friend. He genuinely loves the Lord. He loves the God he some-times doubts. He just happens to be extremely analytical and sees details that most people never see (or care to see, for that matter).

A lesson in finitude

A few years back, I was sitting in my backyard pondering my faith when I began thinking about my ornamental plum tree. I began asking questions like, How deep are the roots? How much water does this tree require to stay healthy? How tall will this tree grow? How many leaves can it hold at a time? During a windstorm with fifty mile per hour winds, how many leaves would fall off? How far would the leaves travel? How many people nursed this tree to health at the nursery? What were their names? How much more water does this tree require now that it's mature compared to its more nascent stages? And on and on and on my questions sprouted as I stared at this tree.

About now you're probably thinking, *I'm glad I don't live in your head.* At times I wish I didn't either. But when all my pondering was finished, here's what I concluded: if I can't be 100 percent cer-tain about the details of even my ornamental plum tree, how in the world can I expect to be 100 percent certain about the details of my God and Christian faith? It was a humbling lesson about my own finitude as I realized "I can't even plumb the depths of my plum tree."

Thankfully, certainty has never been the requirement for belief in Christ. Faith is.[22] Not blind faith, but evidential, reasonable, informed faith. Nevertheless, faith is still involved.

....

Certainty has never been the requirement
for belief in Christ. Faith is.

....

Everyone believes in faith

At the end of the day, we're all in the same dilemma as it relates to certainty. And as a result, we all trust in borrowed scholarship somewhere. As the French political thinker Alexis de Tocqueville once wrote, "There is no philosopher in the world so great but he believes a million things *on the faith* of other people and accepts a great many more truths than he demonstrates."[23]

So there you have it. We are *all* incapable of certainty, even the brightest among us. At times I've wished for an aquarium God to make sense of things. A God who resides above in a sky-like tank, where all we have to do is look up to grab our cues from Him. It may stink being finite, but the quicker we realize that we are not God, nor are we meant to be, the faster we can move beyond this problem of demanding 100 percent certainty to legitimize belief.

Assurance versus certainty

At this point, you might be a little discouraged. But don't be. The lack of certainty doesn't mean you're destined to live with your faith continuously in suspicion. Assuage your fears by recognizing the difference between *certainty* and *assurance*. As Christians we can have a great sense of assurance through the witness of the Holy Spirit. And this assurance can *feel* like certainty.

Paul reminds us that God has "put his seal on us and given us his Spirit in our hearts as a guarantee."[24] Furthermore, Paul writes in his letter to the Romans, "The Spirit himself bears witness with our spirit that we are children of God."[25] Paul experienced this assurance in a visceral *and* intellectual way, even writing, "But I am not ashamed, for I *know* whom I have believed, and I am *convinced* that he is able to guard until that Day what has been entrusted to me."[26]

John the apostle also had this assurance of faith, even writing the epistle of 1 John to provide such confidence: "I write these things to you who believe in the name of the Son of God that you may *know* that you have eternal life."[27]

....

> Assurance of salvation is a work of the Holy
> Spirit, and this assurance can comfort you
> when you wrestle with a lack of certainty.

....

Isn't that refreshing? So don't be discouraged. Learn to distinguish between certainty and assurance. This will help you tremendously. Assurance of salvation is a work of the Holy Spirit, and this assurance can comfort you when you wrestle with a lack of certainty. Furthermore, assurance of your faith will enable you to boldly proclaim the gospel. It will also help you to have confidence in your faith and free you to love God more fully. So take heart—while you may not be certain, you can be sure. And that's worth thinking about.

Evidence versus certainty

A lack of absolute proof and 100 percent certainty doesn't imply the lack of evidence.[28] By no means. Christianity is a reasonable faith. Every belief system has its questions, but once the evidence is brought to bear, Christianity provides the best answers overall, leading to a much higher degree of certainty. And it more plausibly answers life's biggest questions about origin, purpose, and destiny than all other belief options. In the end, Christianity best closes the doubt gap by providing the strongest cumulative case.

When doubts lead to worship

It's time we shift from seeking omniscience to beginning to rest in our finitude. This leads us to revel in the God who is omniscient and to celebrate the fact that He can be known. Can we not rejoice in the romance of knowing the God who is infinite and omniscient? Instead of focusing on our gaps, what if we focused on God's lack of them? See the difference? One approach creates angst while the other instills awe and wonder.

When we demand a doubt-free life, we leave no room to please God through faith. The Bible reminds us, "And without faith it is impossible to please him, for whoever would draw near to God must believe that he exists and that he rewards those who seek him."[29]

....

> When we demand a doubt-free life, we leave
> no room to please God through faith.

....

Consider this. If we could compile an exhaustive case for Christianity that proved it with 100 percent certainty, guess what that would imply? There'd be no room for faith. And with no room for faith, there's no room to please God *by* faith. Thankfully, God provides us reasonable evidence to believe and then asks us to trust Him with our unanswered questions.

Can you do that? And besides, why entertain an exodus from Christianity because of all the things you can't understand when there are so many things you *can*. Perhaps that's where our focus should shift—to celebrating and thanking God for the many things we *can* know.

Trigger 3: Life's Injustices

In his book *Night,* Elie Wiesel recounts his experiences as a prisoner at Auschwitz, Buna, and Buchenwald concentration camps. *Night* is so gripping, the *New York Times* describes it as "a slim volume of terrifying power." When I read the book I was struck, like millions of other heart-wrenched readers, by the horror this man lived to recount. I have visited Buchenwald concentration camp, and *Night* added a whole new dimension to my already disturbing experience.

Wiesel recalls the horror of arriving at Auschwitz and coming to terms with the imminent possibility of being incinerated in the crematory. As he anguished, many wept around him, while another Jew recited the Mourner's Kaddish, a prayer for the dead. And in the midst of all this chaos, Wiesel shares how his father uttered out, *"Yisgadal, veyiskadash, shmey raba"* ("May His name be celebrated and sanctified").

Wiesel then says, "For the first time, I felt anger rising within me. Why should I sanctify His name? The Almighty, the eternal and terrible Master of the Universe, chose to be silent. What was there to thank Him for?" He goes on to say:

> Never shall I forget that night, the first night in camp, that turned my life into one long night seven times sealed.
>
> Never shall I forget that smoke.
>
> Never shall I forget the small faces of the children whose bodies I saw transformed into smoke under a silent sky.
>
> Never shall I forget those flames that consumed my faith forever.

Never shall I forget the nocturnal silence that deprived me for all eternity of the desire to live.

Never shall I forget those moments that murdered my God and my soul and turned my dreams to ashes.

Never shall I forget those things, even were I condemned to live as long as God Himself.

Never.[30]

I won't for a second pretend to have an inkling of understanding into the horror Wiesel experienced. And he's not the only one whose faith has been vanquished by similar injustices. But for whatever reason, during seasons of equally agonizing experiences, some arrive at the opposite conclusion. Instead of losing their faith, they actually discover it and deepen it.

....

Instead of losing their faith during seasons of agonizing experiences, some actually discover it and deepen it.

....

I once read that while the bubonic plague claimed the lives of a third of the people from Europe, the other two-thirds kept going to church in the midst of such evil. It was no different in the concentration camps, where some were left with their faith forever incinerated while others departed with a faith unsinged. Some Jews in the camp doubted toward faith, while Wiesel was found doubting toward unbelief. Further into the book, he writes:

As we lay on our cots, we sometimes tried to sing a few Hasidic melodies. Akiba Drumer would break our hearts with his deep, grave voice. Some of the men spoke of God: His mysterious ways, the sins of the Jewish people, and the redemption to come. As for me, I had ceased to pray. I concurred with Job. I was not denying His existence, *but I doubted His absolute justice.*[31]

Staring into the face of evil, Wiesel found his theology of an omni-benevolent God going up in smoke. His faith was turning to ashes right before his very eyes. The *why* questions rendered him confused. Hopeless. Agnostic and full of doubt.

How about you? Does your faith remain intact in the midst of a myriad of injustices around you? Or upon further reflection have doubt and confusion billowed up? Has the word *why* disturbed you beyond repair?

It's true, being a Christian doesn't give you a magic pill whereby you are never troubled by injustice. Job felt it as the evils settled in and he experienced unimaginable pain. I felt it recently when I saw a video of a person being dragged into the streets and brutally stoned with cinder blocks, while people drove by seemingly detached and unconcerned. Perhaps you've felt it while watching the evening news or when your lover betrayed you or after pondering the grim reality of much of the world scene. Even Habakkuk the prophet posed the question "God, where are you?"[32] Maybe that's a question you have asked when encountering some unspeakable evil or some ghastly injustice.

Ours is a world filled with injustice, but thankfully not one without ultimate justice. In time, God will make all things right. In the meantime, we scratch our heads, stand confused, and sometimes weep in the face of tragedy, morbidity, and macabre evil.

....

Doubt travels in two directions. For
some it heads toward faith and for
others it travels toward unbelief.

....

As we now see, doubt travels in two directions. For some it heads toward faith and for others it travels toward unbelief. Yet, we must face the question C.S. Lewis once posed in *Mere Christianity*, "My argument against God was that the universe seemed so cruel and unjust. But how had I got this idea of 'just' and 'unjust'?...What was I comparing this universe with when I called it unjust?"[33] Donald Gowan, in his commentary on Habakkuk, similarly said, "The human demand that God ought to *act* justly is based solely on the conviction that God *is* just."[34]

I think we have our confusions misplaced. When we see life's injustices, our tendency is to blame God instead of the person who committed the crime. I also think our confusion shouldn't rest solely in whether God is just or unjust. It makes better sense for us to stand perplexed by God's sense of *timing* in meting out justice than it does to wonder if He is just. We ask, "What's taking so long, God?" And Scripture couldn't be clearer regarding God's ultimate sense of justice as we'll all stand "without excuse."[35]

It's not as if the problem shrinks by erasing God from the picture. For instance, under an atheistic worldview, where is ultimate justice? I'll tell you. It's nowhere. Under the umbrella of atheism, Hitler could get off scot-free for the deaths of millions by simply pulling the trigger of the gun he held against his head.

So instead of blaming God or seeking to erase God, we must remember that God *is* just. Yet within this framework, His timing for meting out justice may not always make sense. But like Abraham we should be able to confidently declare, "Shall not the Judge of all the earth do what is *just*?"[36]

....

God *is* just, yet His timing for meting out
justice may not always make sense.

....

Interestingly enough, with the rise of the New Atheism there's been an ironic flip of character whereby atheists give God a bad rap and His created ones become His accusers. God, not man, is the guilty one now. We make ourselves the just ones while God is branded as unjust. Richard Dawkins's now famous quote captures this sense perfectly, "The God of the Old Testament is arguably the most unpleasant character in all fiction: jealous and proud of it; a petty, unjust, unforgiving control-freak; a vindictive, bloodthirsty ethnic cleanser; a misogynistic, homophobic, racist, infanticidal, genocidal, filicidal, pestilential, megalomaniacal, sadomasochistic, capriciously malevolent bully."[37]

Dawkins's portrait of God saddens me. I'm pretty sure I speak for the rest of us Christians when I say, "If that's God, I'm not interested either." The truth is, thoughtful Christians would beg to differ and even be able to provide an alternative way to understand the disturbing passages from the Bible that have sparked such incendiary remarks.

Besides, under atheism, where does one even get a definition of just or unjust? Or what is right and wrong? Aren't we just beasts ourselves? Isn't it each man fending for himself? Aren't we all just trying to survive? Isn't that what we are all about?

Words like *just* and *unjust* and *right* and *wrong* all imply a standard. But what's the standard within atheism? As I've said, under the worldview of atheism there is no ultimate justice. And while Dawkins may struggle to understand God's justice, wouldn't you rather *try* to understand it rather than simply dismiss God because His ways are sometimes hard to digest, believe, or even understand?

In a world marred by sin and human finitude, we will encounter many perplexities. But in the midst of our confusion, we must resist the urge to draw the wrong conclusion. It's better to be confused by God's timing for dispensing justice than it is to have no justice at all.

Life is cruel, but God isn't.
And for that I rejoice.

Doubt Reflections

- *In the absence of certainty there's always room for doubt.*
- *Case for case, Christianity best closes the doubt gap.*
- *Like every disease, doubt also has an initial cause.*

Questions for Further Thought and Discussion

1. Bobby said, "Every doubter must ask, 'What's behind my doubts?' What's the source? The root? The trigger?" If you want to get at the root, you've got to dig it up. Why is that so hard to do sometimes?

2. Alister McGrath said, "Doubt is like an attention-seeking child." What do you think he meant by that statement? And if that's the case, how does our doubt need to be handled?

3. In this chapter, we discussed three doubt triggers. Have you ever had an issue with doubt as it relates to one of these three triggers? If so, would you be willing to give an example?

4. The Bible contains some things that we find hard to understand. List some things that Christians should remember that can help provide greater perspective when we encounter bizarre stories in the Bible.

5. Why is demanding certainty such a futile exercise? And why do people struggle to trust God apart from knowing all the details?

6. Reread Richard Dawkins's quote toward the end of the chapter. Take each of his descriptions of God's character and think of stories or instances in the Bible where Dawkins might have associated such debauchery with God. Now, what would you say to him if he spoke those words to you? Would you be able to give a reasoned *contextual* answer?

Chapter 5

DOUBT TRIGGERS: PART 2

*"We live in a culture that has, for centuries now,
cultivated the idea that the skeptical person is always
smarter than one who believes. You can almost be
as stupid as a cabbage as long as you doubt."*

DALLAS WILLARD

*"As to the doubt of the soul I discover it to be false: a mood
not a conclusion. My conclusion is the Faith. Corporate,
organized, a personality, teaching. A thing, not a theory. It."*

G.K. CHESTERTON

My experience with doubt has felt more like an earthquake than a hurricane. At least with a hurricane there's a heads-up that allows you prep time to board up your house and evacuate. Not so with an earthquake. And believe me, growing up in California I've experienced some serious seismic activity. I was in the 7.1 earthquake that hammered Northern California in 1989, as well as the 7.3 earthquake that shook Southern California in 1992, among others. From my experience, here's what I can tell you. There was no warning. No sirens. Nothing. Earthquakes most often are unexpected. And yet, *something* triggers them.

The same is true with our doubts. One moment we're at peace with our faith and the next we're in a panic. Some question drops into our soul and we think, *Could I be wrong about God? The Bible? Jesus? Or even heaven?* And before we know it, we're experiencing internal seismic activity so severe that it feels like the very foundations of our beliefs are crumbling.

Seismologists use the Richter scale to measure the magnitude of earthquakes. Similarly, our doubts vary in degree of severity. Some doubts shake up our faith more than others. But no matter when doubts come, whether small or big, they come unexpectedly, and they meddle with our faith.

> No matter when doubts come, whether
> small or big, they come unexpectedly,
> and they meddle with our faith.

In the previous chapter we unpacked the first three doubt triggers. In this chapter we'll explore several more of these triggers that threaten to weaken our faith. Again, this list isn't exhaustive. Not even close. But I hope it heightens your awareness to the wide array of doubts people encounter.

Trigger 4: Apparent Bible Contradictions

For Bible-believing Christians, apparent contradictions can pose a real headache. If you read your Bible long enough, you're bound to encounter some of these problematic passages. In his book *Jesus, Interrupted,* famed agnostic and New Testament scholar Bart

Ehrman dishes out a litany of what appear to be Bible discrepancies. However, to Ehrman these discrepancies aren't apparent but *actual*. In withering fashion, the *Boston Globe* touts, "For more than a few folks, *Jesus, Interrupted* will be a grenade tossed into their tidy living rooms of religious faith."[1]

Ehrman fires off a host of examples of these so-called contradictions. Here's a sampling:

- "When Noah takes the animals on the ark, does he take seven pairs of all the 'clean' animals, as Genesis 7:2 states, or just two pairs, as Genesis 7:9-10 indicates?"[2]

- "In Mark's Gospel, Jesus tells Peter that he will deny him three times 'before the cock crows twice.' In Matthew's Gospel he tells him that it will be 'before the cock crows.' Well, which is it?"[3]

- "On the third day after Jesus' death, the women go to the tomb to anoint his body for burial. And whom do they see there? Do they see a man, as Mark says, or two men (Luke), or an angel (Matthew)?"[4]

To Ehrman this problem is so insuperable in the Gospels that he says, "To resolve the tension between the Gospels the interpreter has to write his *own* Gospel."[5] Therefore, Ehrman contends, "The Bible makes *better* sense if you acknowledge its inconsistencies instead of staunchly insisting that there aren't any, even when they are staring you in the face."[6] Ehrman's words have triggered seismic activity in varying degrees for some Christians' faith.

....

Apparent contradictions in the Gospels
served as the genesis of my doubts.

....

I'll admit, apparent contradictions served as the genesis of my doubts. I was a student at Dallas Theological Seminary and taking a course on the life of Christ. As part of our homework, we read a harmony of the Gospels that juxtaposed the four accounts side-by-side. Now, I had seen this issue before, but never so forcefully. While reading the Gospels in this way, I began noticing these apparent inconsistencies, and doubt was triggered. The tectonic plates of my mind were shifting, causing me to think, *Wait a second. If the Bible is God's Word, there shouldn't be any errors.*

I wasn't trying to undercut the Bible. Nor was I seeking to be a skeptic. And I certainly wasn't looking to be a heretic. I was simply using my reason and making observations. Aren't disciples of Jesus supposed to ask questions? We don't check our brains at the door when studying the Bible, right?

So what was I to do? I was in the midst of a spiritual earthquake. A "faith-quake," if you will. Here I was, preparing for ministry at a respected evangelical seminary, and angst was consuming me in epic proportions. I wished someone would give me an easy answer to assuage my doubts, but pat answers seldom satisfy. However, through developing a more skilled approach to Bible study, I learned some things that helped me to doubt toward faith.

> Through developing a more skilled approach
> to Bible study, I learned some things that
> helped me to doubt toward faith.

In their book *When Critics Ask,* Norman Geisler and Tom Howe reveal seventeen common mistakes people make that cause them to doubt toward unbelief when they hear claims that the Bible is full of error. I encourage you to read the introduction to their book on how to approach these Bible difficulties, but here are the basic points. The skeleton without the flesh. Seventeen mistakes we must avoid:

Mistake 1: Assuming that the Unexplained Is Not Explainable

Mistake 2: Presuming the Bible Guilty Until Proven Innocent

Mistake 3: Confusing Our Fallible Interpretations with God's Infallible Revelation

Mistake 4: Failing to Understand the Context of the Passage

Mistake 5: Neglecting to Interpret Difficult Passages in the Light of Clear Ones

Mistake 6: Basing a Teaching on an Obscure Passage

Mistake 7: Forgetting that the Bible Is a Human Book with Human Characteristics

Mistake 8: Assuming that a Partial Report is a False Report

Mistake 9: Demanding that NT Citations of the OT Always Be Exact Quotations

Mistake 10: Assuming that Divergent Accounts Are False Ones

Mistake 11: Presuming that the Bible Approves of All It Records

Mistake 12: Forgetting that the Bible Uses Nontechnical, Everyday Language

Mistake 13: Assuming that Round Numbers Are False

Mistake 14: Neglecting to Note that the Bible Uses Different Literary Devices

Mistake 15: Forgetting that Only the Original Text, Not Every Copy of Scripture, Is without Error

Mistake 16: Confusing General Statements with Universal Ones

Mistake 17: Forgetting that Later Revelation Supersedes Previous Revelation[7]

When we make any of these mistakes, we set ourselves up for a major-league doubt crisis. I'd encourage you to take your difficult Bible questions and run them through this grid. Do this, and more than likely an answer will emerge that satisfactorily speaks to your dilemma. But even if not, it's helpful to remember to give the Bible the benefit of the doubt. You can do this by trusting that if you had enough context and lived in ancient biblical culture, these things would make better sense to you. Sometimes the lack of evidence and the time gap between our culture and the culture of the Bible adds confusion. For now, here are some tips for the next time you struggle with doubt as a result of apparent Bible contradictions.

> Take your difficult Bible questions
> and run them through this grid.

First, when you're stumped by the unclear, rejoice in the clear. As Mark Twain once quipped, "It's not the parts of the Bible that I don't understand that worry me. It's the parts I do understand." We shouldn't expect the Bible, which contains sixty-six books written by forty authors in different genres in three languages and on three different continents, to not have, from a human perspective, some apparent contradictions. As Craig Blomberg writes, "Any anthology of sacred literature written in diverse literary genres over many

centuries, and to a wide variety of audiences for many different purposes, will inevitably exhibit apparent contradictions and theological diversity along with some measure of continuity and unity."[8]

However, in the end, what's so jaw dropping about Scripture is
not that it's littered with apparent discrepancies, but how it's laced
with such a beautiful inner consistency. It's not how dissimilar Scripture is, but how similar. Again, careful study and understanding will
clear up *lots* of these surface-level inconsistencies.

Second, remember that your struggle isn't unique. As long as we've
had the Bible, great Christian thinkers have sought to reconcile these
apparent contradictions while passionately continuing to believe.
But the question remains, can all these discrepancies be reconciled
or are we forcing a square peg into a round hole? As Blomberg
also states, "Not a single supposed contradiction has gone without
someone proposing a reasonably plausible resolution."[9] Like a math
problem in school, it's not that it can't be solved. It's just that I don't
understand it yet. Now that's reassuring.

....

> "Not a single supposed contradiction
> has gone without someone proposing
> a reasonably plausible resolution."

....

*Third, familiarize yourself with today's New Testament scholars and
their helpful works.*[10] People like Craig Blomberg, Darrell Bock, Dan
Wallace, Craig Evans, Andreas Köstenberger, D.A. Carson, and
other erudite thinkers have offered viable solutions to discussions
like this.

*Fourth, don't impose twenty-first-century journalistic methods
on an ancient oral culture; rather, learn the ancient culture's acceptable forms of transmission.* In other words, don't come to the Bible

with twenty-first-century presuppositions. As with any document, whether it's the Bible, the Declaration of Independence, the Gettysburg Address, a love letter from your spouse, or an online news article, it has to be read with the historical context in mind.[11]

Fifth, don't drive yourself crazy trying to memorize answers to every apparent contradiction. Rather, learn the tools for reconciling apparent contradictions as you arrive upon them. Not to minimize the importance of this work, but unless you're called to be a biblical scholar, trying to memorize the answer to every apparent contradiction will prove to be quite vexing. I'm sure you can use your time better in the prayer department or pursuing other more faith-enriching endeavors. Like bumps in the road, just take them as they come.

Trigger 5: The Problem of Suffering and Evil

Ours is a world filled with both moral and natural evils. *Moral evils* refer to things like murder, rape, theft, adultery, and child abuse. These evils are the result of fallen mankind's free will, and many people have doubted God's goodness because of man's cruelty. Philosophers and theologians also refer to *natural evils,* such as the volcanic destruction of Pompeii, hurricane Katrina, the Thailand tsunami, and the bubonic plague.

Catastrophic events leave a wake of insurmountable pain, confusion, and, yes, *doubt.*

All these evils remind us that our world is dysfunctional. It's not our final home. Catastrophic events leave a wake of insurmountable pain, confusion, and, yes, *doubt.* And each worldview has its own explanation or rationalization for suffering and evil. Buddhism claims evil is just an illusion and all of us are in need of nirvana. Hinduism calls on karma to explain suffering and evil. Atheists see evil and suffering as a brute fact of our deterministic existence.

However, the Christian views suffering and evil altogether different. To the Christian, both moral and natural evils are the result of living in a sin-cursed world—a world that God warned Adam and Eve about back in the Garden of Eden, informing them that life would be very unpleasant if they disobeyed His Word. But disobey they did. And it's been a history of unpleasantries ever since.

It may not be the explanation we like, but it's our explanation. It also gives us a window into God's heart. From Adam and Eve's experience, we learn that in order for us to be truly free, we must possess the ability to receive or reject God and His ways. And yet, even with our sin and rebellion, His sovereign grace and mercy have provided a way to bring our evil and suffering to an end. Every believer has the hope of a renewed paradise. A paradise of perfection no longer under the taint of sin.

Interestingly, this very problem of evil and suffering, more than any other issue, became the Achilles' heel that led to Bart Ehrman's apostasy. For Ehrman, it is inconceivable to reconcile a good God with a world filled with such evil and despair. How could a loving God allow for such anguish? In the preface to his book *God's Problem*, Ehrman writes:

> The problem of suffering became for me the problem of faith. After many years of grappling with the problem, trying to explain it, thinking through the explanations that others have offered—some of them pat answers charming for their simplicity, others highly sophisticated and nuanced reflections of serious philosophers and theologians—after thinking about the alleged

answers and continuing to wrestle with the problem…I finally admitted defeat, came to realize that I could no longer believe in the God of my tradition, and acknowledged that I was an agnostic.[12]

The problem of suffering blew out what was left of the already flickering flame of Ehrman's Christian faith. Today, his faith is nothing more than a personal footnote, a mere vestige of his past.

> God's timing is not likely to be my timing. The delay on God's behalf doesn't mean He won't act.

I too can look at the world of suffering and think, *God, where are You? Aren't You going to do something?* But then I remember that if God truly is infinite in every way, His timing is not likely to be my timing. The delay on God's behalf doesn't mean He won't act. The real problem is I don't see *all* the issues at hand. He does. I don't understand the multilevel domino effects and interconnectivity of millions of events. He does. My sight is limited. His is not.

So I remind myself, "You're not God, Bobby." And I trust that God is good, just, loving, and one day will set all things right. For every person whose faith has been weakened by abysmal circumstances, there are others whose faith has brought them through the darkness.

Furthermore, in light of my sinful nature, there is an even greater problem—the problem of *good*. I don't want to minimize suffering, nor am I backpedaling on evil, but for most of us, the good we enjoy far outweighs the bad. Every parent who rejects God on the grounds that our world is racked by suffering needs to ask, "Why then are we bringing children into this evil world?" Wouldn't that make every parent evil too? But most parents know that though the world is broken, it's a place where we can still experience blessing.

....

The bigger question in light of our fallen
nature is why isn't there *more* evil?

....

The bigger question in light of our fallen nature is why isn't there *more* evil? Why is it that we want to take credit for the good and cast all blame for evil at the feet of God? Isn't that backward? Aren't we reversing things a bit here? Isn't it God's goodness that prevents us from completely destroying ourselves? As the eminent New Testament scholar N.T. Wright so aptly put it, "Evil may still be a four letter word. But so, thank God, is love."[13]

Trigger 6: The Weight of Unconfessed Sin

Unconfessed sin is a guaranteed way to decrease our faith and increase our doubts. And the longer we fail to confess our sin, the harder and more impenetrable our hearts become. Hard hearts not only create hearts of doubt, they can also lead to hearts of unbelief. And that's scary. We cannot dismiss the importance of the lost art of confession. The author of Hebrews writes this sobering warning to his fellow believers:

> Take care, brothers, lest there be in any of you an evil, unbelieving heart, leading you to fall away from the living God. But exhort one another every day, as long as it is called "today," that none of you may be hardened by the deceitfulness of sin. For we have come to share in Christ, if indeed we hold our original confidence firm to the end.[14]

The author tells us that sin is not only deceptive, but it carries with it certain heart-hardening viruses. When we fail to take confession seriously, we allow our hearts to harden. And callous hearts pave perfect paths for doubt and unbelief.

> Callous hearts pave perfect paths
> for doubt and unbelief.

Trigger 7: Internet Bloggers

In our sound-bite culture, we are too quick to deem as worthy the less than credible platform some have made for themselves. I'm thinking of certain bloggers who clog up cyberspace with their opinions that are not supported by sound research. Many writers blog their thoughts in a stream of consciousness that in turn gets stamped as authoritative by undiscerning readers and people more interested in flare than facts. The Bible is often the direct target of such bloggers, and many professing Christians have had their faith painfully tested because of them. These believers plummet into doubt, all because they lack the discernment to handle some amateur armchair theologian's elementary attacks against Christianity.

Typically these bloggers twist the words of Scripture to justify their claim that the Bible promotes slavery, genocide, the inequality of women, and so on. However, they are uninformed about what the Bible really teaches. Anyone can take verses out of context and create a crisis in someone who doesn't know the real story. Let me go on record saying that if the Bible really glorifies slavery, genocide, and the inequality of women, then I'm out. I'll join the bloggers in their corporate anthem.

However, that's not the case. There's a lot involved in being a faithful interpreter of Scripture, not the least of which is time and training. My advice is not to put a lot of stock in Internet bloggers who are without credentials. Any self-proclaimed "thinker" with a computer can spout their nonsense to the world. But trusting in their scholarship, opinions, and conclusions is like trusting in the medical skills of a trick-or-treater in a doctor's costume.

That's. Not. Smart.

Instead, investigate to see if they have any credentials and training to support their claims. Then check their conclusions against well-regarded teachers and scholars. Certainly many bloggers are worth reading. But as great as the Internet is, it opens its doors to anyone and everyone, from solid Bible teachers to heretics.

Trigger 8: Failing to Radically Seek God

When we refuse to radically seek God, we open ourselves up to a faith crisis. It's through our pursuit of Christ that we experience a relational *connectedness*. When Christianity becomes merely a head game all about finding the next answer to our most pressing questions, something inside of us dies relationally. God wants more for you than just a life of trying to figure Him out so you can place Him in a theological box.

> When Christianity becomes merely a head game all about finding the next answer to our most pressing questions, something inside of us dies relationally.

What would you prefer from your spouse, parent, friend, or child? To be analyzed or to be loved? To be examined or appreciated? Christ calls us to love God with our entire being.[15] Think of it like this: God is not an object to be analyzed, but a Savior to be adored.

Christianity is not a mind game. It's a life spent in pursuit of Christ. Knowing Him. Loving Him. Adoring Him. And yes, trusting Him. If we're not careful, we will detach our heads from our hearts and reduce our faith to a lifelong Q&A session. But it's bigger, better, and much more than this.

Be careful to not compartmentalize your faith by seeking God only with your mind. Seek Him with your *entire* being. All of you in pursuit of all of Him. That's the way the Christian should roll. We're created to love God and to know Him.

Intimately.

Passionately.

Wholeheartedly.

Therefore, it's crucial that we fan the flame of our affections for Him. As God told Jeremiah, "You will seek me and find me, when you seek me with all your heart."[16]

....

It's crucial that we fan the flame
of our affections for God.

....

Every day we fail to seek God is a day we choose to open ourselves up to doubt. Selah.

Trigger 9: A Misguided Relationship to Prayer

It was important to Jesus that His disciples understand prayer. On one occasion, shortly after Jesus finished praying, one of His disciples approached Him and said, "Lord, teach us to pray."[17] And Jesus jumped at the opportunity.

I've found prayer to be one of life's greatest enigmas. I've enjoyed wonderful, fulfilling seasons of prayer, while at other times I've been deeply perplexed by it. Here are some things that can potentially trigger doubt in the believer as it relates to prayer.

First, believing false teaching on prayer can create spiritual confusion and doubt. "Name it and claim it" preachers want you to believe that if you just have enough faith, you can have whatever your little heart desires. Many people have bought into this lie only to end up utterly disillusioned. This prayer formula causes us to treat God like our servant. We end up acting like His master, dishing out our commands, and all in the name of our misplaced faith.

Second, thinking God's on board with our request, only later to be disappointed when it doesn't work out. I can relate. There have been times in my life that I sincerely thought God was leading me in a certain direction only to discover a door bolted shut.

Third, assuming that since God knows everything, it's a waste of time to pray. Many proclaim, "Why bother praying since God knows what's going to happen anyway?" Or, "Prayer is a waste of time since what will be, will be." But that's not Christianity. It's fatalism. And it robs us of any relationship with God. It helps me to remember that if Jesus, being perfect, valued His prayer life, how much more should we? For Jesus prayer was much more about His relationship *with the Father* than it was about getting His needs met.

....

If Jesus, being perfect, valued His prayer
life, how much more should we?

....

Fourth, wrongly projecting our desires on God, which sets us up to experience blown expectations and, in turn, tempts us to doubt. It's important that we pray according to Scripture. Otherwise, we may assume God values the same things we do. Besides, let's be real. We've got way too many "*pamper* me prayers" and not enough "*transform* me prayers." Our job is to fall in alignment with Scripture rather than to persuade God to get on board with our wishes. The majority of prayer is just getting our will to agree with God's. And that takes surrender. And surrender doesn't come easy. Isn't that the truth?

Fifth, at times God's seeming detachment, disinterest, and slowness to respond triggers doubt. Habakkuk the prophet felt perplexed by God's sense of detachment. He cries out, "O LORD, how long shall I cry for help, and you will not hear?"[18] I love Habakkuk's authenticity before God. He lays it out there. He shares what he *feels.* What he *thinks.* No holding back.

I once heard someone say, "Bobby, we need more Jewish prayers in the church today." What this person meant is we need more authentic, vulnerable, honest prayers. The kind you read in the Psalms, where the psalmists wrestle through their doubts, confusions, and fears in a very vulnerable way before God. I'm talking about full-disclosure prayers. We need to take even our doubts to God in prayer. Church must be the place where we can feel safe enough to get real. Raw. Fully disclosed. Instead, we think, *What if I mess something up? What if I don't pray right?* So we pray these cheesy, fabricated prayers that lack authenticity.

....

Half of working through our doubts is just getting real with each other and with God.

....

Not Habakkuk. He was authentic *to the core* with God. I've said before that transparency is my survival medicine. Half of working through our doubts is just getting real with each other and with God. During one massive doubt-quake, I wrote this out to God:

> God, I'm struggling. Deeply. In my heart I'm wondering, Is this true? Are You even there? Am I typing on a blank page or into Your listening ear? It's as if I hear voices in my head. Voices that come packaged in the form of questions, saying, "Is this all a joke? Have I been deceived?" And voices that hijack my peace, saying, "Leave this thing. Walk out of the box of Christianity and look at it from the outside. See how trapped you are. See how gullible you've been. You've been duped." But it's not like I want to doubt. Unless I'm just deceived about that too. Doubts have sapped my passion, my joy, and my sense of purpose. At times I feel like I'm hanging off a cliff perched up on the heights of ministry success and holding on by my fingernails. I'm no longer on the foundation, but I haven't let go either. I'm in that no-man's land, that place between faith and unbelief. Living in a world of doubt. At times existing. Some moments, I think, "I can't hold on much longer." God, this is where you come in. I need to get up on the rock and see that *You're* my Rock, because if I'm left to my own strength, I'll soon let go. And the consequences won't be pretty. God, I beg You to be real in my life. Show Yourself faithful. Remove the doubt triggers and flood me with faith. Faith to believe in You afresh. I plead with You to help me. I'm in the quicksand of doubt this morning and it's now up to my neck. I need an intervention. I need You— *now.* I'm a truth seeker. That's what I want. I just want to walk in the truth. You say You're the truth—show me the truth. I beg You.

Have you ever felt this desperate? If so, have you really laid it out there? Frankly, I'd rather hide this from you. Remember, I'm not only a Christian, I'm a pastor. And I'm not only a Christian pastor, but I'm also a Christian apologist. I'm supposed to have it all together, right? But I don't. So, in the meantime, I doubt toward faith.

Shortly after this journal entry my wife walked into my office. And strangely enough I felt better. You might ask why. Because there's something about being real with God *and* others that has a calming effect. A little assurance from the outside can create peace on the inside. I guess that's why.

There are those moments when my Christian faith makes perfect sense and other moments where it all appears to be nonsense. But that's all they are—*moments*. Moments that require waiting, relating, reflecting, praying, and trusting. And in each of these moments when doubts trigger, we must persevere, even if it seems like God's on vacation. He's not. As Jesus once said, "I am with you always, to the end of the age."[19]

Next time a doubt is triggered, try resting in that.

Doubt Reflections

- *Doubt is more like an earthquake than a hurricane. It often comes unexpectedly.*

- *Hard hearts not only create hearts of doubt, they can also lead to hearts of unbelief.*

- *Every day we fail to seek God is a day we choose to open ourselves up to doubt.*

Questions for Further Thought and Discussion

1. Bobby said, "If we're not careful, we will detach our heads from our hearts and reduce our faith to a lifelong Q&A session." How can we avoid doing that?

2. Of the doubt triggers that Bobby mentioned in this chapter, which one can you relate to the most?

3. In the past two chapters, nine doubt triggers have been briefly examined. Can you think of any other things that trigger doubts?

4. Bobby described doubt by saying it's more like an earthquake than a hurricane. Can you relate? If so, in what way?

5. Why do you think it's so hard to be totally real with God and each other? What are the risks involved?

6. Is there a particular struggle with doubt that you are having that we can pray for today?

Chapter 6

FOUR FACETS OF DOUBT

*"Doubts are the ants in the pants of faith. They
keep it awake and moving."*

FREDERICK BUECHNER

*"Doubt is the secret sin buried deep within our souls. We
are all afraid to touch it, to unloose the monster. But
authentic Christian belief demands that we uncover
it, name it, understand it, and make peace with it."*

KELLY JAMES CLARK

Doubt is a multifaceted diamond. It's complicated. Like art…or even like my bride. I've told Heather on several occasions, "I'll never get to the bottom of you." That's because she's a delightful mystery. Wonderfully complex. An enigma. Unsolvable. A multifaceted lady. I totally get why the Bible commands husbands to live with their wives in an "understanding way."[1] There is a certain complexity about a woman. She's not a problem to be solved but a person to be understood. Try to solve a lady, and she'll feel like you're trying to conquer her. Instead, it's the very *mystery* of a woman that helps a man continue his pursuit of her. And that's what every woman truly wants—to be *pursued* by her man.

Obviously, we can't fully compare our wives to doubt lest we end up in the doghouse...or worse. But we can agree that they're both multifaceted and, as with my wife, I must learn to live with doubt in an *understanding* way.

Doubt comes in several shades, what I call the "four facets of doubt." By understanding the different facets, we will be better equipped to target our doubts and deal with them more precisely. These facets of doubt can slowly erode our faith, rendering us spiritually impotent. With that in mind, let's explore together these four facets.[2] Like choosing paint colors, it's sometimes hard to distinguish between them.

Emotional Doubt

Perhaps nothing paralyzes a Christian's once vibrant faith more than emotional doubt. This facet of doubt is brutal. It wears you down, and at its peak it can bring you to the utter end of yourself, drowning you in despair. And when life twists us up like that, we can end up turning our frustration Godward.

> Emotional doubt is brutal. It wears you down.

It's at this point we must ask a very important question: "What is behind my emotional doubt?" Interestingly enough, tucked beneath the covers of emotional doubt is a wide array of underlying possibilities. These *sub-emotions* can be torturous.[3] Emotions like *fear* cause us to wonder, "What if my belief is a mere fantasy? What if I'm not really saved? What if God doesn't forgive me for the affair

I'm having right now?" Or *anger* that declares, "How dare God take my spouse away from me." Or, "What kind of God would lead me to start a business only to watch me fall flat on my face." Or, "How could God allow my child to be diagnosed with cancer?"

Another sub-emotion that creates doubt is *worry*: "Will God provide for our financial needs? What if I stay single my entire life? What if I lose my job?" *Depression* is another underground emotion that wonders, "Why did you make me this way, God?" Or we think, "I'll never be accepted?" Or, "My life feels useless." Or we ask, "Why am I such a failure, God?"

Even emotional *confusion* can cause doubts as we ponder the perplexities of our dismantled world. Out of this confusion we utter, "If God is good, why does He allow so many people to die each day of starvation?" Or, "How can God really care about children when so many of them are orphans?" This confusion creates emotional doubt when life fails to make sense. And the puzzle remains the puzzle.

Often our reaction to emotional doubt is as multifaceted as doubt itself. We can be peculiar little creatures at times in the way we respond. Emotional doubt makes us want to quit, run, lash out at others, self-destruct, hide, and perhaps even die. No doubt, emotional doubt is vexing. And if you've experienced this form of doubt, you can relate. You know what it feels like. So do I. You're not alone here.

....

Emotional doubt arises when we experience
or hear about something that is hard to
reconcile with a good and loving God.

....

Generally, emotional doubt arises when we experience or hear about something that is hard to reconcile with a good and loving

God. And it's in wrestling through the problem of suffering and evil where we feel the full force of emotional doubt. Philosophers distinguish between the *intellectual* problem of evil and the *emotional* problem of evil. The intellectual problem seeks to show that it's not illogical for God and evil to coexist in our present state. Granted, while the idea may not sit well with us, it's not self-contradictory.

The emotional problem of evil is much harder to stomach. It creates in many a distaste for God. While one may intellectually come to see that God and evil can be logically reconciled, the emotional problem may linger, leaving some to conclude, "Something still doesn't smell right about this." It's at this point that we seek to express our emotional confusion. It's the "Why God?" in all of us that leads us to feel as if God doesn't care. It's here we find ourselves asking, "God, if You're good, why do You allow so much evil? Why not prevent this mess?"

Christian apologist William Lane Craig describes in graphic detail a story that stirred up the "Why" question. Back in the eighties, Craig saw a news story about a huge mudslide that swept over a village in another nation. A little girl was tragically trapped in the muddy floodwaters up to her chin, and for some reason rescue teams couldn't free her. Craig shared how this young girl just stood there stuck in the floodwaters and constantly spit out the muddy water. Evening after evening the news would return to this story only to discover the girl's plight was growing worse. Dark circles formed under her eyes as she became physically exhausted. "We were watching her *die* right in front of us on television," Craig said.

It appeared as if God was unaffected. Unconcerned. Indifferent. As if He was ignoring what was going on. Tragically, the newscaster came on one evening to announce that the little girl had drowned. During such abysmal suffering Craig found himself saying, "God, how could You permit this little girl to suffer? If she had to die in the mudslide, let her drown quickly, but why this pointless lingering death?" Then he said, "When I see things like this, I have to admit it makes it hard for me to believe in God."[4]

What Craig experienced was a serious case of *emotional* doubt. Yet he was quick to admit that such emotional trauma doesn't give us a *real* reason to dismiss the existence of God. The truth is that as long as we live in a world where free-willed creatures exist, there has to be a potential for evil, lest we be mere automatons. But it may take time for our emotions to catch up with that truth. Thankfully, we're *not* automatons. And while we may not comprehend God's reasoning, it doesn't mean there is no reason.

> While we may not comprehend God's reasoning, it doesn't mean there is no reason.

Consider for a moment the suffering caused by our sin. Though God doesn't condone sin, He is so great that even in our sin He reveals something about Himself that would've stayed forever concealed *experientially* had it not been for that sin. For example, without sin, how would we know that we are unconditionally loved? We have to break the conditions to know we're unconditionally loved. Not only that, but had we not experienced sin, we wouldn't know that God is forgiving and merciful. What is there to forgive or show mercy toward in a world absent of sin? What is forgiveness and mercy in a perfect setting?

Or think about God's justice. Had there been no injustice, we would not comprehend the true nature of justice itself. Such qualities as unconditional love, forgiveness, mercy, and justice are showcased against the black backdrop of our sin. Think about it. God is so great that even when we rebel against Him, He has a way of revealing more of His eternal greatness.

Multiple angles of God's magnificence break through when we look at humankind's original sin in the Garden. This doesn't mean that God allowed us to sin *so that* He could flex His divine muscles and show off more of His attributes. No. A simple reading of Scripture makes it quite obvious that He warns us over and over and over again not to sin. God's not like some insecure middle schooler seeking attention. However, it's because He is so good that we can draw out these observations of His ineffable goodness to begin with. And there's more.

Our emotions can be well served when we remind ourselves intellectually that even though we live in an evil-ridden world filled with sin and suffering, this reality cannot negate the actuality of God. Like the doctor who may inflict his patient with pain in order to provide a greater good, so too we must trust that God has His reasons for allowing suffering, *though those reasons are often unseen.* He may allow suffering to wake us up from our complacency, to teach us greater dependency, to develop compassion or forgiveness in us, or to help us trust in His unseen plan.

> God has His reasons for allowing suffering,
> though those reasons are often unseen.

Frankly, how can we become like Christ unless we learn to forgive? And how can we forgive unless we've been hurt? So it's very possible that God allows us to be hurt for the greater privilege of becoming like Christ. And when we are racked with confusion as a result of our pain and suffering, we discover the greatest comfort of all by realizing Jesus also suffered. His death on a cross for our sins brings forgiveness to us. Eventually, He will bring an end to suffering and evil by destroying the works of the devil.[5]

Paul wrote to the church in Rome, "Suffering produces endurance, and endurance produces character, and character produces hope."[6] Notice the progressive cause-effect relationship here. As we suffer we must choose to endure. And as we endure something amazing happens. Character is produced. And as we observe this character formation taking place, we are infused with hope.

....

> One day all suffering will end, and we'll
> encounter our ultimate hope realized in God.

....

Take hope, Christian. When we suffer, often our first response is to get out of it instead of asking *what can we get out of it*. And there is a difference. One day all suffering will end, and we'll encounter our ultimate hope realized in God. An eternity where our emotions are finally made whole. Glorified at last. For that we await—with hope.

Intellectual Doubt

We experience intellectual doubt when we struggle to find an answer to a question we've stumbled upon. The questions that plague the intellectual doubter can feel insurmountable and can also paralyze their relationship to Christ. We've all heard the statement, "The more you learn, the more you realize how much you don't know." Very true. That's why so many new believers are extremely bold and passionate. They don't even know what questions to ask *yet*. But in time, if they're eager learners, they'll accumulate their own set of questions.

Sometimes it seems that for every book I read, I learn of ten others that I need to read. And for every question I chase down an answer for, I end up collecting another dozen in the process. The number of questions begins to snowball, outgrowing our ability to find all the answers. During those times it may seem easier to simply do nothing at all, to take a break in our search for answers. But that's not the way we move forward. At least not long term.

With an increasing number of unanswered questions, how does a Christian keep his passion for Christ intact? After an interview I did with Hank Hanegraaff on *The Bible Answer Man,* he offered some helpful advice for living with the tension of so many unanswered questions. He encouraged me to celebrate my finitude: "Instead of being crushed by a gigantic snowball of questions, let your questions increase your awe for God. If we could figure God out, He'd be a pretty small God." That resonated with me.

> "Instead of being crushed by a gigantic snowball of questions, let your questions increase your awe for God."

Currently I'm reading *The Old Testament Documents: Are They Reliable and Relevant* by Walter Kaiser. In it Kaiser draws attention to the fact that the book of Jeremiah exists in a shorter and a longer version among the manuscripts we possess. Immediately we respond, "What?" That's the cry of intellectual doubt being born. And we may find our once-unshaken faith in Scripture coming into question. We realize that this whole canonical process wasn't as crisp as we might prefer.

Though there are lots of situations like Kaiser's example above, what else would we expect when dealing with thousands of years of human history? But I've found that when I take the time to chase down these enigmas, I can find a satisfactory answer to my questions. In the case of Jeremiah, Kaiser reconciles the complexity:

> The dual form of Jeremiah could possibly be explained by the fact that Jeremiah did have to compose two forms of this text due to the infamous and outrageous actions of the Judean king, who unceremoniously cut up each section of the scroll as it was originally read to him and tossed into the fire. Thereupon, records Jeremiah 36:32, "Jeremiah took another scroll and gave it to the scribe Baruch son of Nariah, and as Jeremiah dictated, Baruch wrote on it all the words of the scroll that Jehoiakim king of Judah had burned in the fire. And many similar words were added to them."[7]

What you'll find as you continue to search out questions like this is that, though manuscript copying and canonization were at times messy, there is sufficient archaeological, literary, and manuscript evidence to give us intellectual confidence in the reliability of both Old and New Testament documents. There is an explanation for most, if not all, of these enigmatic problems.

> There is sufficient evidence to give us intellectual confidence in the reliability of both Old and New Testament documents.

Sometimes there is a fairly obvious answer, while at other times there's not. Sometimes we have to dig. Concerning the longer edition of Jeremiah, Kaiser says, "Here is strong evidence for an expansion of the original composition of the book of Jeremiah."[8] To me this is a nice example of what often happens. We learn something, perhaps feel a bit uneasy, then we seek out the answer and finally arrive at a plausible explanation. But through the process we're becoming a greater defender of the faith.

So take heart. When you come across these intellectual forks in the road, don't be alarmed. Step back, take a deep breath, remember there *are* explanations out there, and learn to enjoy the *process* while continuing to grow closer to God.

Ministerial versus magisterial use of reason

As we search and explore, we must be careful not to read the Bible as if it's guilty until proven innocent. This is one sure way to turn our faith into a cold, pure science. And our relationship with God will die as the romance fades.

Martin Luther, the well-known reformer, referred to this as the difference between a *magisterial* use of reason and a *ministerial* use of reason. Someone who practices the former places himself above the Scriptures and judges whether it is true or false. That person becomes the final arbiter of truth and error. However, the person who practices the latter submits himself under the Scriptures, trusting the Word of God as the final arbiter of truth. This is what Augustine referred to as "faith seeking understanding."

....

If we wait until we have all the answers
to our questions before we can believe,
we'll never believe anything.

....

This isn't intellectual suicide. And if we wait until we have all the answers to our questions before we can believe, we'll never believe anything. The atheist continues to believe in his atheism regardless of his unanswered intellectual questions. Every honest atheist must concede that something coming out of nothing does sound pretty silly. And I'll concede that manna falling from heaven for forty years also sounds silly. But it's intellectually more feasible to believe in a God who provides manna from heaven than to believe that nothing produced the entire known universe out of nothing.

As it's been said before, "Out of nothing no thing comes." Besides, if Genesis 1:1 is true, then we can certainly handle all the other miracles that may stump us. If "In the beginning, God created the heavens and the earth" is true, then baking up a little manna is mere child's play for God.

Volitional Doubt

The third facet of doubt is volitional doubt. By volition, I'm speaking of our *wills* or the ability to choose. The will is that component of our personality that doesn't naturally surrender. Volitional doubt is experienced when there is a battle between God's will and ours.

You find yourself in a crisis of belief, wondering, "Does God really know what's best for my life? Can I trust Him to lead me in the right direction? What if I follow Him only to regret it later? Is it possible my life would be better off if I just made my own decisions?"

And besides, who likes surrendering their will? Letting go. Loosening the grip. Relinquishing control. *None* of this comes naturally. Yet, so much of the Christian life involves surrender. It's about yielding and about dying to self. Indeed. The very essence of faith is about surrendering our will to God's will. And what makes it all the more difficult is that discovering God's will isn't always as clear or as easy as we would like.

> The very essence of faith is about
> surrendering our will to God's will.

At times we can *feel* or sense God's guidance through the inner promptings of the Holy Spirit. We can even *see* God's will through circumstances. And we can also *hear* God's will through the body of Christ and especially through learning Scripture. But as we process what we *feel, see,* and *hear,* we must confidently ask, "Does this all align with the Bible?" That's what keeps the Christian centered and living biblically.

Living scripturally aligned

Our job as believers is to read the Word and then align our lives to it. Scripture contains God's will in written form. That doesn't mean we read the Old Testament Levitical laws and then apply them in the same way to our lives. By no means. Keep your pet lamb alive. We are under the *New* Covenant.

> Our job as believers is to read the
> Word and then align our lives to it.

But that doesn't mean all that's contained under the Old Covenant is useless for the Christian. The key is to ask, "What are the timeless principles in the text before me and how does it apply to my life?" A good book on biblical interpretation (or hermeneutics) can help you learn how to connect the dots, bridging the ancient text to our own culture.[9]

While speaking recently to one of my close friends, I said, "The best thing that can happen in my life between now and when I die is that I learn to live in alignment with more books of the Bible." By saying this I was acknowledging that I need to surrender more of my will to Scripture. And guess what? It's really hard to surrender to God's Word if we don't know His Word.

I fear that many Christians avoid the Bible because they'd rather *not* know all that it demands. They'd rather live in ignorance, living their way. Perhaps that describes you, shying away from God's Word in the name of securing your own will. Like others you may think, *Why would I want to know more about God's will? What if it runs contrary to mine?* Well, in that case you'd experience a clash of the wills. And volitional doubt would likely ensue. So that's why it's easier for some to just avoid God's Word rather than deal with the challenge to our will that comes along with it. God's divine pokes can feel like an irritant. A nuisance. But we need to realize that His pokes and prods are merely His *sacred invitations* into closer relationship with Him. Welcome the invitation.

Christian sanctification is all about becoming more like Jesus. And Scripture is the manual where we learn how this is accomplished. In fact, Jesus is the One who fulfilled all Scripture. More than that, He embodied it. Lived it. Walked it. And taught it. Jesus is the Word of God—made flesh. And that's where true change takes place. Where metamorphosis is realized. Where new creation living takes on real-life fulfillment. We aim to become like *Him* in virtue.

....

Christian sanctification is all about becoming
more like Jesus. And Scripture is the manual
where we learn how this is accomplished.

....

The problem is that the volitional doubter struggles while simultaneously second-guessing God. Jesus modeled the surrendered life beautifully when He cried out in the garden of Gethsemane, "Father, if you are willing, remove this cup from me. Nevertheless, not my will, but yours, be done."[10] The anthem of the volitional doubter might be, "Nevertheless, not Your will, but *my* will be done."

In His great Sermon on the Mount, Christ taught us to pray, "Your kingdom come, your will be done, on earth as it is in heaven."[11]

That's where the Christian icing is found. In doing God's will. In crying out, "Your kingdom come, your will be done." In surrendering.

So exactly *how* do we surrender to God's will? How do we yield? Here's a little advice for you the next time you encounter a battle of the wills.

First, get honest with God. Tell Him why you're wrestling to surrender your will to Him. Jesus modeled this deep vulnerability before the Father, and so can you. Process your struggle through wide-open prayer. I've heard it said, "Half of all prayer is just getting our will out of the way." What's keeping it in the way to begin with? Talk to God about it. Open yourself to a little guidance, prayer style.

Second, ask God to give you the strength, courage, and perspective to surrender your will to His. Sometimes our desires are so strong, running contrary to God's will. And that makes it brutally difficult to surrender. We feel tangled up and stuck.

The unhappily married man can't stop thinking about his secretary who appears to like him. The emotion is so powerful that it feels like magic, and he can't imagine letting go. But then, in comes the Intruder. And what does He say? "Don't do it. Surrender. Trust Me, it's not worth it. You'll destroy your life." And oh, how the battle racks him. He feels paralyzed. He wrestles, saying, "But God, You don't understand."

But He does.

He's God. And when it comes to understanding, I think God's got us one-upped. We can take comfort in that. Life is filled with difficult choices. But no one can make those choices for us. God has allowed us the freedom *and* the ability through the Holy Spirit to make those hard, daily decisions. Take courage, God will supply us with the strength we need to do His will. As Paul told the Philippians, "I can do all things through him who strengthens me."[12] If Paul can overcome while chained in prison, so can we. We're empowered by the same God.

> Take courage, God will supply us with
> the strength we need to do His will.

Third, once you surrender, stay surrendered. In writing to the Romans, the apostle says, "I appeal to you therefore, brothers, by the mercies of God, to present your bodies as a living sacrifice, holy and acceptable to God, which is your spiritual worship."[13] You've probably heard the saying, "The problem with living sacrifices is they crawl off the altar." Isn't that the truth? We surrender our will to God and then think, *On second thought...* But there is no second thought after we surrender our will to Him. We must choose to stay on the altar, trusting God to lead us His way.

Evidential Doubt

The final facet of doubt is evidential doubt. The person voicing evidential doubt sounds something like this: "Is there enough evidence to believe that Christianity is true? How can I know the evidence hasn't been tampered with? How can I wade through all the contradictory evidence of church history to arrive at a sense of what's real? And doesn't belief in Christianity just grow more problematic with the passing of time? With two thousand years of church history, don't we now have more people who have polluted the trail to truth? So how can I know which authorities to trust when several of them contradict each other? Aren't we far too removed from the composition of Scripture to ever be confident that our faith could be reasonably grounded? And what's the right amount of evidence? When is enough, enough? When is my search project complete?"

And on and on and on. The evidential doubter collects questions like beachcombers collect seashells. And like the ocean before him, the questions feel endless and seemingly inexhaustible.

....

The evidential doubter collects questions
like beachcombers collect seashells.

....

If your doubt is of this particular facet, then next time you're overwhelmed with questions, press pause and remember a few things.

First, every belief system has its questions. Asking questions is part of the human story. We are rational beings who think, reflect, refine, and wrestle through our existence to better know truth. The real question is, which set of beliefs best answers life's weightiest questions? This is where Christianity can rise to the challenge for the believer.

Second, it's obvious that omniscience isn't achievable for us, so we shouldn't bother striving for it. That'd be a waste of time and an exercise in futility. We don't have to collect every seashell in order to understand seashells.

Third, just because we're not omniscient doesn't mean we're doomed to a life of agnosticism. It's actually okay to be agnostic (ignorant, lacking in knowledge) about some things, but we don't have to be agnostic about everything. Even the agnostic believes some things.

> It's actually okay to be agnostic about some things, but we don't have to be agnostic about everything.

Fourth, while Christianity doesn't answer all of our questions, it does answer the essential ones sufficiently. Questions about the existence of God, the resurrection of Jesus, the rise of the church, and many other pertinent questions about our faith can be answered with reasonable evidence for the faith-seeker.

Fifth, we should refuse to be all or nothing in our approach to truth. One of the dangers with some streams of evangelicalism is a rigidity that leaves no room for mystery, inquisitiveness, ambiguity, and theological tensions. They contend, "The mature Christian is the one who can put all the pieces together," and they will brand us if we don't agree with every belief contained inside their doctrinal box.

The problem is, if we're a thinking person, we're going to refine certain doctrines and our understanding about them throughout our lifetime. That doesn't mean there's something wrong with us. It just means we're thinking. And to suppress the doubts that come as a result of such thinking is to suppress thinking itself. Doubt is not something we want to suppress. Rather, our doubts must be brought out of the closet and analyzed in order to be dealt with and put in their proper place.

I'm tired of the "don't think, just believe" brand of evangelicalism. This hasn't served the church well. It's through thinking that we are able to believe. God never bypasses the mind on His way to the heart. He designed us to think, reason, and search. And based on the evidence He provides, we can confidently believe.

> God never bypasses the mind on His way to the heart. He designed us to think, reason, and search.

Don't be afraid of tension in your belief or of not fully understanding everything. But also don't fear the confidence and clarity that can come when you work through the haze of doubt. There *are* things that we can know with an unshakeable confidence.[14]

This "don't think, just believe" mentality has produced a lazy batch of Christians who are often high on opinions and low on awareness and reasoning. The answer to the questions that threaten this type of Christian is often to just preach louder. Be more defensive. Act more arrogant. And yet, they often remain blind to their own theological blind spots.

Have we not read *The Emperor's New Clothes*? Just saying.

Seeing the Big Picture

Something that helps me when I struggle with evidential doubt is to step back and look at all the evidence we do have. We can get so lost in the weeds that we feel like we're losing our way. When this happens, it's helpful to focus on the abundant evidence at our disposal rather than obsess over what we *don't* have. I find it comforting to know that our faith can be philosophically, scientifically, and historically grounded.

For example, teleological, cosmological, and moral arguments all point to God's existence. The *teleological* argument, for instance, argues that apparent design in the universe can be traced to a Designer. This can be observed by exploring the fascinating discoveries that have surfaced in DNA, complex life forms, and even the universe itself.

David, the ancient psalmist, saw design pointing beyond itself to God when he wrote, "The heavens declare the glory of God, and the sky above proclaims his handiwork."[15] Furthermore, Paul writes to the Romans, "For what can be known about God is plain to them, because God has shown it to them. For his invisible attributes, namely, his eternal power and divine nature, have been clearly perceived, ever since the creation of the world, *in the things that have been made.* So they are without excuse."[16]

Paul constructs these words to those who suppress their belief in God to show that there is no excuse for not believing in Him. The only reason some have failed to notice is because they chose to ignore the clearly revealed evidence of God's created order. The evidence is right there, in the sky, written large and in all caps. It's *in* creation. It's *in* you and me. The evidence is all around us like lyrics everlastingly exclaiming, "This is not an accident."

The Bible merely affirms what theistic philosophers have long said to be true: God exists. By starting with the question, "What evidence is there for God's existence?" we can find assurance by becoming familiar with these varying arguments.

After considering the philosophical evidence for God's existence, consider also the *historical* evidence for the life, death, burial, and resurrection of Jesus. The implications of the resurrection are huge. In fact, the Christian faith hangs on it.[17] The evidence for the resurrection is confirmed by grasping the ramifications of the empty tomb, His post-resurrection appearances, and the rise of the early church. How else can you explain the transformation of the fearful disciples who abandoned Jesus during His earthly life? Why would they go on to die for Jesus unless the resurrection was an historical event? They saw something. They saw *Him*. Alive.

For the Christian, the validity of our belief rises and falls on the resurrection. Without it, we have a nice story about a good man that ended in tragedy. But in the face of the overwhelming evidence, I simply can't explain away the resurrection. I've even tried—not because I wanted to disprove it, but just to test the strength of the arguments. I was TKO'd.

> For the Christian, the validity of our belief
> rises and falls on the resurrection.

The resurrection seals the deal for me. And from this event I can rewind to the earthly ministry of Christ and find confidence in my Bible because Jesus affirmed the validity of Scripture. If the resurrection happened, then Jesus is indeed God because He claimed to be so and the resurrection in turn justified His claims. And if He's God, then the Word of God is true because He believed it. In this sense, truth produces a domino effect where one truth impacts another in an unbroken chain.

More than that, Jesus also promised the coming Holy Spirit to lead His followers into all truth. There is so much I could get into here. But the point is that my doubts are relaxed when I consider how Jesus Himself affirmed the Scriptures.[18] He affirmed the historicity, the miracles, the law and the prophets, and even perceived Himself as the fulfillment of Scripture as the promised Messiah.

So now I'm back to the Bible. Back to where I often get lost in the weeds. Back to where I began. But because I believe in Jesus and Jesus believed in the Bible, it helps me to trust in Him. Every

Bible-believing Christian believes their Bible in part on good evidence and in part by trusting that if Jesus believed, then they can too.

We have extrabiblical evidence for some parts of the Bible, as in the case of the resurrection. This evidence helps confirm our biblical belief. And then there are other stories, such as Jonah and the fish, that seem almost fantastical...and yet Jesus affirmed them. And His affirmation helps us to embrace those portions of the Bible that seem ridiculous or "hard to swallow." So, I reason, if Jesus affirmed the entirety of the Old Testament with His first coming, I trust that He will affirm the New Testament with His second coming. In the meantime, I'll rely on a Bible that has proven itself to be reliable and earned the right to be trusted.

In this chapter we discussed four different facets of doubt. In the next chapter, we'll look at the *root* of doubt as it relates to Satan and spiritual warfare. I suppose it could even be called "The Fifth Facet" as spiritual doubt is certainly another facet of doubt. But it's more than a facet. It's a root that we must unearth to understand.

Doubt Reflections

- *Doubt is like a multifaceted diamond.*

- *God never bypasses the mind on His way to the heart. Scholarship must not be detached from relationship.*

- *Perhaps nothing paralyzes a Christian's once vibrant faith more than emotional doubt.*

Questions for Further Thought and Discussion

1. What stood out to you the most from this chapter?

2. Volitional doubt can feel like a big wrestling match with God. Bobby said, "The anthem of the volitional doubter might be, 'Nevertheless, not Your will, but *my* will be done.'" Can you share an example of a time when God brought you to a place of surrender?

3. Bobby mentioned four facets of doubt. Can you think of any other facets?

4. Which facet of doubt gives you the most amount of trouble?

5. Bobby said, "Tucked beneath the covers of emotional doubt is a wide array of underlying possibilities." Why is it so important to identify the sub-emotions behind our emotional doubt?

6. If Jesus rose from the dead, that settles it. Do you believe that? That is, do you think everything rises and falls on the resurrection of Jesus Christ? If so, how can belief in the resurrection help quiet your doubts?

Chapter 7

THE ROOT OF DOUBT

*"But doubt is wily and cunning and never, as
it is sometimes said to be, loud or defiant. It is
unassuming and sly, not bold or assertive—and
the more unassuming, the more dangerous."*

SØREN KIERKEGAARD

*"It's hard to believe always but more so in the world we
live in now. There are some of us who have to pay for
our faith every step of the way and who have to work
out dramatically what it would be like without it and if
being without it would be ultimately possible or not."*

FLANNERY O'CONNOR

I once heard an eerie story about a lady who became concerned for her pet snake. *Pet* and *snake* are two words that should never be used together. I hate snakes. If you think Indiana Jones loathed them, I do even more. Anyway, we're not talking about a dinky garter snake. No, it was a big, long python. And why was she so disturbed? Apparently, the poor snake wasn't eating, so she sought out her veterinarian for a little advice.

"By any chance does your snake sleep with you?" the vet asked.

"Funny you should ask," the lady said. "Yes, my snake does sleep with me." (Are you believing this?)

"The reason your snake doesn't eat," her veterinarian said, "is because it's sizing you up as it purposely starves itself, waiting for the opportune moment to consume you."

Talk about sleeping with the enemy.

> Satan wants nothing more than to
> consume us and our faith.

Whether this story is really true or not, like that snake, Satan also studies us and knows us better than we know ourselves. He wants nothing more than to consume us and our faith. That's exactly why Peter encourages us, "Be sober-minded; be watchful. Your adversary the devil prowls around like a roaring lion, seeking someone to devour."[1]

As Christians we are in the midst of a war. A *spiritual* war. And this war can be tricky to detect. That's because it's a war that takes place in an unseen world. The apostle Paul wrote, "For we do not wrestle against flesh and blood, but against the rulers, against the authorities, against the cosmic powers over this present darkness, against the spiritual forces of evil in the heavenly places."[2]

> We must treat our doubts as frontline
> attacks from the enemy.

That means we must treat our doubts as frontline attacks from the enemy. Far from the caricatures of Satan that look like Gene

Simmons dressed up in a red suit and holding a pitchfork, Satan and his demonic host are powerful spirit beings. They deceptively align around a common goal: *to destroy our faith*. I can't stress this enough. The evil one wants to stretch our doubts until at last they snap, resulting in unbelief.

Enter Satan

When dealing with Satan, we should neither overestimate him nor take him too lightly. In the preface of *The Screwtape Letters*, C.S. Lewis reminds his readers to avoid two errors regarding the demonic world,

> There are two equal and opposite errors into which our fallen race can fall about the devils. One is to disbelieve in their existence. The other is to believe, and to feel an excessive and unhealthy interest in them. They themselves are equally pleased by both errors and hail a materialist or a magician with the same delight.[3]

How true this is. For some people there's a demon behind every bush. For others there's no such thing as the demonic world. It's purely superstition. Instead of these extremes, our goal should be to properly estimate Satan. And this starts by becoming familiar with him.

The Bible depicts Satan as a created angelic being who rebelled against God along with a third of the angelic realm. Since that time, Satan and the fallen angels (aka demons) have remained in complete opposition to God and are on an all-out mission to usurp everything God represents. Satan is not an all-powerful, all-knowing, and ever-present being. He's not equal to God in any way. Rather, he is a created being with limitations. Nevertheless, he is far more powerful and knowledgeable and aware than we can possibly imagine. He's a force to be reckoned with, and we should not make light of him.

> Satan is a force to be reckoned with, and
> we should not make light of him.

Take a look at depictions of him in Scripture and you'll quickly discover that he is dark. Evil. Nefarious. And criminal. Paul refers to him as "the god of this world" who "has blinded the minds of the unbelievers, to keep them from seeing the light of the gospel of the glory of Christ, who is the image of God."[4] Jesus referred to Satan as "a liar and the father of lies."[5] Matthew calls him "the tempter."[6] He's even called "the deceiver of the whole world."[7]

Fortunately, his end is written in ink. Literally. The Bible tells us that Satan's destiny has already been determined, and at the end of the age he will be cast into the eternal lake of fire.[8] In the meantime, he plans to wreak havoc in the church and in you and in me. So listen up.

"Has God Said?"

Satan's deep hatred toward the human race began with humanity's first pair: Adam and Eve. It's there, in the Garden of Eden, where we encounter the serpent seeking to unravel Eve's faith with his doubt-shaped question, "Indeed, has God said...?"[9]

> A dreadful drama is unfolding and Satan is
> enticing Eve to doubt toward *unbelief*.

Now, if you're a doubter, you may have a hard time getting past a talking snake. I get it. It's weird. And there are lots of helpful commentaries you can delve into on this topic. This is not the place. For now, let's not miss the bigger picture of what's happening. A dreadful drama is unfolding and Satan is enticing Eve to doubt toward *unbelief*. In her conversation with the serpent, she's encountered the epitome of anti-god. Read these verses for yourself because it's here that you'll discover the *root* of doubt. In Genesis 3 we read:

> Now the serpent was more crafty than any other beast of the field that the LORD God had made. He said to the woman, "Did God actually say, 'You shall not eat of any tree in the garden'?" And the woman said to the serpent, "We may eat of the fruit of the trees in the garden, but God said, 'You shall not eat of the fruit of the tree that is in the midst of the garden, neither shall you touch it, lest you die.'" But the serpent said to the woman, "You will not surely die. For God knows that when you eat of it your eyes will be opened, and you will be like God, knowing good and evil." So when the woman saw that the tree was good for food, and that it was a delight to the eyes, and that the tree was to be desired to make one wise, she took of its fruit and ate, and she also gave some to her husband who was with her, and he ate. Then the eyes of both were opened, and they knew that they were naked. And they sewed fig leaves together and made themselves loincloths.[10]

These verses are tragic and devastating beyond our imagination. Don't be fooled into thinking the entire human race was forever hosed just because the first woman did a little fruit tasting. That's what we call missing the forest for the trees. It's so much bigger than that. It's not about the fruit. It's about a heart that rebelled against God and sided with Satan. It's a tale about doubting toward unbelief.

About being deceived. About putting our desires before God's. It's about rejecting God's Word in order to go our own way.

Satan's Tactics to Devour Us

So with that in mind, lets excavate several nuggets from this ancient narrative—some real-life lessons to help us battle doubt. Let's begin by becoming familiar with the tactics Satan uses to unravel our faith. To devour us.

> We need to become familiar with the tactics Satan uses to unravel our faith. To devour us.

First, Satan is crafty in the way he distorts God's Word. As Old Testament scholar Bruce Waltke puts it, "Satan's craftiness is seen in his cunning distortion of God's words. With subtle guise, the adversary speaks as a winsome angelic theologian."[11] Paul the apostle doubly attests to Satan's craftiness saying, "Satan disguises himself as an angel of light."[12] He doesn't show his cards. He didn't show up to Eve and say, "Hey, I hate God and everything about Him, and I'm on a mission to trump His ways. Wanna join me?" No, he's much more calculated. He's not reactive but rehearsed. He's not impulsive but intentional. He knows his game plan, and he'll gladly recruit you—deceit and all. He's wise as a serpent but far from being harmless as a dove.

Richard Baxter, the seventeenth-century English Puritan church leader, writes,

> The devil is a greater scholar than you, and a nimbler disputant: he can transform himself into an angel of light to deceive: he will get within you, and trip up your

heels before you are aware: he will play the juggler with you undiscerned, and cheat you of your faith or innocency...You shall see neither hook nor line, much less the subtle angler himself, while he is offering you his bait. And *his bait shall be so fitted to your temper and disposition,* that he will be sure to find advantages within you, and make your own principles and inclinations betray you; and whenever he ruineth you, he will make you the instruments of ruin to others.[13]

That's haunting. And calculated. But that's how Satan rolls. And that's why we must stay alert.

Second, temptations to doubt can come when we least expect them. Eve wasn't searching for doubt. But perhaps she was experiencing a strong case of the *curiosities,* contending, "Why can't I have a little snack off the old Tree?" We can't know for sure. But we do know that Eve is enchanted upon encountering this unexpected intruder in her Garden home. In hindsight, I'm sure she thought, *How did this happen so fast? How could I have been so blind? So deceived? So hoodwinked?*

It's the same for us. One moment we're enjoying a little paradise and the next we're questioning God's Word. Life can be that way. And it's exhausting. Satan plants the "Has God said?" question into our mind, and it quickly takes root. And before we know it we're doused with doubt. These "Has God said?" moments can come out of the blue, so as believers, we can't drop our spiritual guard.

....

Satan plants the "Has God said?" question
into our mind, and it quickly takes root.

....

I've experienced my share of "Has God said?" moments. Recently

I was driving my son Dawson to school. It was just another day in paradise. But when we passed an old graveyard, I suddenly sensed the ancient serpent whisper, "Do you *really* believe the dead are going to come out of those graves someday?"[14] At once, I found myself trying to visualize what that would look like, only to find myself thinking, *That is weird, isn't it?* It just seems so foreign to my modern mind. And out of nowhere this thought disrupted my emotional state. Intellectual doubt turned to emotional doubt. I went from paradise to the pits just like that.

> I sensed the ancient serpent whisper, "Do you *really* believe the dead are going to come out of those graves someday?"

I had to go back to the Scriptures and concede that though I don't fully understand, I still believe. Sure, I wish everything in Scripture made perfect sense to me, but this side of heaven it won't. So I reason that if God created our bodies to begin with, then He can certainly re-create them anew in the resurrection.

But this is how Satan can unwind us. And before we know it we're all tangled up in doubt. Twisted up in intellectual anxiety. One glance at a graveyard and the next thing we know we've gone from serenity to emotional suffering. And it's in that moment when our doubt will head one direction or the other. Toward belief or unbelief. That's another reason why we must stay on guard.

Third, Satan persuades us to doubt God's goodness. He wants us to think that God is holding out on us, cheating us out of the good stuff in life. That's exactly what he did with Eve, saying, "You will not surely die. For God knows that when you eat of it your eyes will be opened, and you will be like God, knowing good and evil."[15] Satan completely flips God's Word. Adam and Eve were to avoid the tree of the knowledge of good and evil *not* because God was holding out, but because God was *protecting* them.[16]

Satan dresses himself up like the good guy, and Eve's about to fall for it. Adam too. According to Scripture, during this temptation scene Adam was right there with Eve, passively standing by.[17] He wasn't reminding Eve of what God *actually* said. He wasn't protecting her, leading her or fighting for her.

Humanity's fall was a joint decision. A team choice. Adam was all in. Both caved in to temptation mouth first. Eve and her husband were lured by the lust of knowledge and personal fulfillment. It's as if Adam was saying "ladies first," only it wasn't out of gentlemanly chivalry but out of deceitful cowardice. They couldn't stand the mystery of not knowing. They wanted a little eye-opener, and that's exactly what they got. They wanted to be like God, to experience *certainty* like Him. Obeying God's restrictive ways seemed silly, so they took the bite, which became history's most horrific moment. It's been graphic ever since.

Fourth, realize that spiritual doubt is not the result of our environment; it comes from within. Think about it. Adam and Eve were living in a perfect context when all this transpired. We may think, *If only I had a better life or I lived in a better setting, that would fix all my problems.* But doubts, sin, and rebellion are not the products of a bad environment. We can live in the Mojave Desert, on a beach in Tahiti, in the Swiss Alps, or in the city of our choice, and we'll quickly discover that we can't avoid our doubts. That's because our enemy is a traveling salesman, going wherever we go to peddle his lies. Here's something worth chewing on. If Adam and Eve could doubt in paradise, how much more are we susceptible to doubt in paradise lost?

Ultimately, Satan would like to massacre our
love for God by suffocating us with doubts.

By subverting God's Word, Satan triggered doubt in Eve, causing her to wonder if God was holding out on her. She became convinced that God was limiting her life. And once intoxicated with an
appetite for rebellion, she was right where Satan wanted her. Like
a master hypnotist, the great serpent also yearns to undermine our
confidence in God's Word. He wants to tweak and twist our theology, painting God in a negative light. Ultimately, he'd like to massacre our love for God by suffocating us with doubts.

*Fifth, Satan never shows us the consequences, only the short-term
fleshly "benefits."* He keeps our attention on the present, revealing
only the short-term satisfaction we'll receive.

After Eve became convinced that God was holding out on her,
she took another look at the tree: "So when the woman saw that
the tree was good for food, and that it was a delight to the eyes, and
that the tree was to be desired to make one wise, she took of its fruit
and ate, and she also gave some to her husband who was with her,
and he ate."[18]

What just happened here? Adam and Eve lost sight of keeping
God's Word and instead caved into their cravings, going for what
was a "delight to the eyes" and reaching for what would "make one
wise." Little did they realize that in doing so, they played the fool
and failed to see the consequences coming their way. "Then the eyes
of both were opened, and they knew that they were naked. And they
sewed fig leaves together and made themselves loincloths."[19]

I'm convinced that in their post-fall existence, Adam and
Eve were the most miserable people to ever live. They knew they
could never get back to the Garden. They went from perfection

to imperfection, and through the rearview mirror, they would always lament the choice they had made. That one choice changed everything.

But for us, we move from imperfection toward perfection, and as we look back to our pre-Jesus days, we can see progress from then to now. Growth. Life-change. We say, "Thank God, I'm not what I once was." Through the reflective mirror of our personal history, our progress gives us hope. Adam and Eve experienced perfection, only to lose it. We started off in imperfection and look to gain perfection in our eventual glorification.

Sixth, when faced with the choice between doubting God's Word and believing it, we should always choose belief. I can hear Adam and Eve's justifications: "But this doesn't make sense. What a silly little command. What's wrong with a little appetizer off the branch? I mean, it's just a bite." And little by little they grew wise in their own eyes. To them, God's ways seemed absurd.

> We can't bend God's Word to make it more palatable. Instead, we receive all of His truth, even the parts that are hard to digest.

But when we take a bite of the forbidden fruit—when we diminish God's Word in order to justify our tastes—it also takes a bite of us. Choosing to believe God's Word, even if it seems petty, is the action we must choose. We can't bend His Word to make it more palatable. Instead, we receive all of His truth, even the parts that are hard to digest.

Eve had a choice to make that day. A choice between belief and unbelief.

In his beautiful yet gut-wrenching book, *A Severe Mercy*, Sheldon

Vanauken writes how he comes to the end of himself before looking to God with daring belief. In a letter to C.S. Lewis, he writes,

> I choose to believe in the Father, Son, and Holy Ghost—in Christ, my lord and my God. Christianity has the ring, the *feel*, of unique truth. Of *essential* truth. By it, life is made full instead of empty, meaningful instead of meaningless. Cosmos becomes beautiful at the *Centre*, instead of chillingly ugly beneath the lovely pathos of spring. But the emptiness, the meaninglessness, and the ugliness can only be seen, I think, when one has glimpsed the fullness, the meaning, and the beauty. It is when heaven and hell have *both* been glimpsed that going back is impossible. But to go on seemed impossible, also. A glimpse is not a vision. A choice was necessary: and there is no certainty. One can only choose a side. So I—I now choose my side: I choose beauty; I choose what I love. But choosing to believe *is* believing. It's all I can do: choose. I confess my doubts and ask my Lord Christ to enter my life…I do not affirm that I am without doubt, I do but ask for help, having chosen, to overcome it. I do but say: Lord, I believe—help Thou mine unbelief.[20]

Wrestling through his own doubts, Sheldon chose belief. Belief in God. Belief in His Word.

Seventh, we need to straighten out twisted truth by combating it with total truth. We can't protect ourselves with God's Word until we first know God's Word. Instead of being deceived by Satan, both Adam and Eve should've reminded him of what God had really said. Instead, their lusts blinded them, and they believed a lie rather than the truth.

This is exactly how Satan tried to bring Jesus down in the wilderness. He approached Him with twisted truth, but Jesus countered Satan's lies with total truth. Three different times Satan tried to tempt Jesus, and each time the Lord replied, "It is written...It is written."[21]

Have you ever played Whac-A-Mole? Once the game starts, you wait eagerly for the moles to pop up so you can hammer them back into their holes with your mallet. The more moles you whack, the higher your score. Fighting off doubts can feel a bit like playing Whac-A-Mole. Once you knock one doubt down, another doubt pops up.

> Fighting off doubts can feel a bit
> like playing Whac-A-Mole.

This wearisome process has sapped countless doubters. We need to become so familiar with the aroma of God's truth that we can sniff out error when it's presented to us. Satan wants to give us a customized version of the Bible. He uses Scripture all the time, but he fashions it to fit his own likings and purposes. And if we hear a voice that says "Has God said?" we should realize we're about to be duped. Let's prepare ourselves well, combating twisted truth with total truth.

Eighth, we shouldn't dismiss the reality of the unseen world. It's real, present, and powerful.

Before I went into full-time ministry, I experienced an unforgettable season of spiritual warfare. It was as if I were being dragged through the horror of the unseen world in order to never forget that it exists.

> Before I went into full-time ministry, I experienced
> an unforgettable season of spiritual warfare.

After losing my appetite and several pounds, I also lost hope of ever feeling normal again. I booked an appointment with a medical clinic to find out what was wrong with me. I remember telling God before the appointment that I didn't care what the problem was, I just wanted it detected so I could start treatment that would help me feel normal again. I was surprised when they gave me a clean bill of health. The only issue was my slightly elevated blood pressure. It was as if nothing but God's power could fix this trial. My emotions seemed to be utterly inflamed as I anguished through this hopeless suffering. This all occurred in my early twenties.

Allow me to rewind a moment and give you a little context. Just a few years prior to this I heard the gospel for the first time. I was nineteen years old. Soon after that I placed my saving faith in Jesus Christ. The first year and a half as a believer was a difficult season as I struggled to abandon my old party lifestyle. But all this would change on October 9, 1994, when I attended my first AA meeting. I went on to attend over four hundred meetings in my first year of sobriety. Yes, at times more than one a day. I wasn't the skid row kind of drinker, but I was a young, hard partier, and as a result I created painful consequences for myself. And for whatever reason, I simply couldn't give up drinking on my own. I needed help. I could see where that life was going to take me if I didn't act fast.

After I got clean, my life took on new meaning. I began channeling my addictive personality Godward. I was sold out. I was in God's army sharing my faith with everything that moved. And the enemy didn't like it. The more I lived for God, the more intense the warfare became. I sensed that Satan's minions were on an all-out assault to bring me down.

At a loss for how to navigate my way through this intense spiritual warfare, I spoke to an elderly Christian woman I worked with at the Ritz-Carlton Hotel in Dana Point, California. After hearing my symptoms, she said, "Bobby, I think you're going through spiritual warfare." I had never heard that term before, but after she explained what it was, things started to make sense.

About a week later she showed up at work with a cassette tape in her hand (now you know this was a long time ago), handed me the tape, and said, "I believe this is for you." She told me the tape showed up in her mailbox after our conversation. She hadn't ordered it and she couldn't figure out why it came to her house. That is, until she opened it and saw that it was titled "Spiritual Warfare" by Brian Broderson (who is now at Calvary Chapel, Costa Mesa, California). As a newbie to the faith I devoured Broderson's exposition of Ephesians 6. He drew on other scriptural examples to show how Satan seeks to cripple believers through fear, worry, depression, condemnation, and *doubt*. During this season, I experienced all the above. That's why this was such a difficult time of my life. Nevertheless, this would become one of the most important sermons I ever heard in my life. I must have listened to that tape a dozen times or more.

....

Becoming aware of Satan's ways enabled
me to engage the battle and not remain
blinded to what was happening around me.

....

There's so much more we could discuss here, but over time, through simply becoming aware of Satan's ways, I was able to engage the battle and not remain spiritually blinded to what was happening around me. I learned in a deep way that the unseen world is real and it's powerful. Now, anytime I struggle with doubts about the unseen world, all I need is a little reflection time. As a pastor, I couldn't afford to do ministry unaware of this. I guess the Lord wanted me to experience a little bit of it myself. I still do at times. But now there's hope. And that makes all the difference.

Satan's Goal

As you can see, Satan and his minions exist to sabotage every ounce of our faith and weigh us down in the false assurance of unbelief. We must not let that happen. Do you remember Jesus's words to Peter? "Simon, Simon, behold, Satan demanded to have you, that he might sift you like wheat."[22] And what exactly was it that Satan wanted to sift? Peter's faith. And how do we know that? By noticing what Jesus said next. He comforts Peter with these words: "But I have prayed for you *that your faith may not fail.*"[23]

Is it any surprise that Satan wanted to dismantle Peter's *faith*? Of course not. And tragically, Peter, engulfed by fear, denied Jesus three times. Unbelievably, his denial happened just hours after he had emphatically told Jesus in the upper room that he'd never deny Him, even saying, "If I must die with you, I will not deny you."[24] Satan wants our faith to fail too. He longs to grind our doubts down until we're left in the dust of unbelief.

> Satan longs to grind our doubts down
> until we're left in the dust of unbelief.

That's why Paul wrote, "So, if you think you are standing firm, be careful that you don't fall!"[25] This is a full-time battle. There's no time to drop our guard even if we think we're off the frontlines. There's no guaranteed break from this battle. Satan doesn't care if we're tired, hurting, confused, or fed up. That's why we must stay suited up in the armor of God.

After reminding us that we are in a spiritual battle, Paul admonishes us, "Therefore, take up the whole armor of God, that you may be able to withstand in the evil day."[26] Paul then lists the Christian weaponry the believer must be armed with, stressing our need for truth, righteousness, prayer, and in particular *faith*. Paul writes, "In *all* circumstances take up the shield of *faith,* with which you can extinguish all the flaming darts of the evil one."[27] Among Satan's weapons are *doubt darts* aimed at destroying our faith. So we need to keep our shield up because Satan is a cruel master. He will use doubts, fears, anger, lust, gossip, or even overconfidence to extinguish our faith. Like Peter, we desperately need to be covered in Jesus's prayers. And fortunately, Jesus is all in as it relates to praying for His followers. In fact, the Bible calls Him our great intercessor.[28]

> Jesus is all in as it relates to
> praying for His followers.

Several years ago I heard about a missionary couple who lived in a hut in some obscure village. One day they entered their home, only to encounter a massive viper. Of course, they got out of there as fast as they could. When their neighbor heard about it, he grabbed his machete and, while the couple waited outside, entered the hut. The couple grew worried when they heard lots of noise, as if all hell were breaking loose inside their hut. At last, their neighbor came out, but the racket inside continued. Seeing their confused faces, the tribesman told the couple, "Don't worry, the snake is dead. He just doesn't realize it yet." Apparently, the snake had been decapitated and was swinging its body in all directions, slapping things all over the place. I guess you could say it was wreaking a little havoc before its time expired.

That reminds me of the garden story in Genesis 3 and the words of Scripture,

> "I will put enmity between you and the woman,
>   and between your offspring and her offspring;
> he shall bruise your head,
>   and you shall bruise his heel."[29]

As God laid out the consequences of the fall to Satan and to Adam and Eve, we learn that Satan's head would eventually be crushed. And in time that's exactly what happened. On the cross Jesus crushed the head of the serpent, meting out a deathblow. Satan is finished. Decapitated. The hourglass is emptying and he knows it. In the meantime, he's just wreaking a little havoc. Until then, "Submit yourselves therefore to God. Resist the devil, and he will flee from you."[30] Don't let that old serpent bully you around with doubt any longer. And never forget that "he who is in you is greater than he who is in the world."[31]

Doubt Reflections

- *If Adam and Eve could doubt in paradise, how much more are we susceptible to doubt in paradise lost?*

- *You must treat your doubts as frontline attacks from the enemy.*

- *The evil one wants to stretch your doubts, until at last they snap, resulting in unbelief.*

Questions for Further Thought and Discussion

1. What did you find most interesting in this chapter?

2. What can we learn from Jesus's temptation in the wilderness about fighting off Satan in the midst of spiritual warfare?

3. Bobby shared a brutal season of spiritual warfare that he went through. Have you ever tangibly experienced spiritual warfare? Or is this language new for you?

4. Bobby said, "Satan never shows you the consequences, only the short-term fleshly 'benefits'." Elaborate on what you think he meant.

5. How has the culture so caricatured Satan as to make Christians feel silly talking about him? And does seeing him as a created, powerful, spirit being help lessen that for you?

6. In this chapter we learned that Satan and his minions aren't to be overestimated nor underestimated, but properly estimated. What does this mean to our everyday life as Christians?

Chapter 8

NAVIGATING DOUBT

"A man was meant to be doubtful about himself, but undoubting about the truth; this has been exactly reversed."

G.K. CHESTERTON

"The only way to doubt Christianity rightly and fairly is to discern the alternate belief under each of your doubts and then to ask yourself what reasons you have for believing it."

TIMOTHY KELLER

Have you ever been hopelessly lost? It's a horrible feeling, isn't it? When I was four years old, we were living in Laguna Beach, California. Ours was a quaint little home, perched high up in the bone-dry hills of South Orange County. From our family room we had a picturesque view of the Pacific Ocean. We could even catch a stunning shot of Catalina Island on a clear day. The view from the back deck was just as spectacular. It was as if the whole world was before my very eyes.

One day I decided to go for a little walk by myself. Once outside, I crossed the street in order to make my way into the brush-filled hills. Something went terribly wrong on my walk. I was too short to see over the bushes, and I felt like I was trapped in a maze that I could never escape. My walk of curiosity turned into panic as fear overwhelmed me. I thought to myself, *How will I ever get out of here?* At last, with my little heart racing, I finally found a way out. I was never so excited to see asphalt, the street that paved the way home for me. To my safe spot. In an instant, my panic turned to peace. I was no longer lost. At last, I was home again.

When I struggle with doubt, I can sometimes feel like that four-year-old lost boy all over again. I feel alone. Fearful. Panic filled. And I wonder, *Will I ever get out of here? And if so, how?* Doubt can be a dark place. And like a maze of bushes, it can disorient us.

> Doubt can be a dark place. And like a
> maze of bushes, it can disorient us.

In this chapter, I'll help you navigate your way through your doubts. Every doubter needs a navigation system for their doubts. An inner GPS. A sense of direction. As long as we feel lost, life will seem hopeless. But finding something solid will turn our panic into peace. This chapter promises no magic formula. No five-step process. No miracle-working prayer. No mystic chant. It's simply a troubleshooting chapter, enabling us to wrestle through our doubts more intentionally. In the end, I'm just one doubter telling another doubter how to find faith. Let's consider these navigation tips and try to get ourselves *unlost*.

Rank Your Doubts

First, grab a memo pad or your laptop and start listing your doubts. Then group them into macro categories. For instance, you may discover that most of your doubts have to do with one of the following macro areas: the problem of evil, God's existence, the reliability of Scripture, miracles, or even pluralism. Each of these *macro* areas has a myriad of *micro* questions attached to them. If you're a heavy-duty doubter, you've identified lots of micro-level questions that now need to be grouped under one of your macro categories.

After doing this, you are now ready to rank your doubts according to priority. This project allows you to see where your doubts are most burdensome and vexing. If you did this exercise...*congratulations*. You just created your own personal study guide. Rather than getting lost in the weeds, now you can step back and tackle one category at a time. This approach will focus you, helping you begin discerning your doubts more clearly.

Embrace Doubt as Your Frenemy

Bizarre but true, doubt can serve as a good friend, even though it usually feels like an enemy. It's a matter of perspective and how we handle it. While Satan uses doubt to destroy us, God can use doubts to develop us. Here are several benefits that doubt can produce:

- Doubts can deepen our dependence on God.

- Doubts can drive us out of complacency as we eagerly search for answers.

- Doubts can cultivate Christian humility within us as we realize that everything isn't so black-and-white after all. Doubt has a way of softening the rigid, inflexible literalist.

- Doubts can help us relate to other doubters with more compassion. Jude even reminds us to "have mercy on those who doubt."[1]

- Doubts can equip us to be a sharper Christian apologist in our quest for answers.

- Doubts can help us grow in Christian discernment as we sift through what to believe and what not to believe.

- Doubts can serve as a necessary reminder that our battle is not against flesh and blood. The root of this soul war is spiritual. And it's very powerful. Indeed.

- Doubts can create in us a greater longing for heaven, for that day when our doubts will vanish. Paul said, "Now I know in part; *then* I shall know fully."[2] What a day that will be!

It's no wonder some have referred to doubt as not just a friend but also a gift. The gift of doubt. Imagine that. It sure doesn't feel like a gift, does it? We must learn to embrace doubt as our *frenemy*. The friend side of this word urges us to find the benefits of doubt and the enemy part reminds us that doubt can break us, if we let it.

> The gift of doubt. Imagine that. It sure doesn't feel like a gift, does it?

So refuse to let your doubts jettison your faith. Rather, let them fuel it.

Avoid Thinking That Says, "If You Doubt, You Must Not Love God"

It's quite possible that the very fact you're so woefully depressed by doubt is not because you don't love God; it's because you do. If you didn't love Him and if your beliefs didn't matter to you, then these doubts wouldn't hurt so bad. You wouldn't be plagued. A person of genuine faith will experience not only mental torture from intellectual doubt but also emotional torture. It metastasizes. The nominal believer is the one who remains emotionally unaffected by doubt. To him, it's all in his head. The nominal believer may be a bit confused, but he's certainly not hopeless.

Don't Overly Obsess Over Your Doubts

Remember what we said earlier, "Doubt is like an attention-seeking child: when you pay attention to it, it demands that you pay even more attention."[3] This is a vicious cycle that is difficult to escape from. Simply put, if we feed our doubts, they'll grow. Some people obsess while others *overly* obsess, and their doubts become all-consuming. It's possible to become so fixated on our doubts that we feel locked inside them. Yet we don't feel safe, especially since we don't even know the combination to get out of our confinement. We just feel stuck. Trapped like a chained prisoner. But that's what obsessions do. Every time we obsess over our doubts, we pave the way for those doubts to possess us. Doubter, beware—if you fixate on anything long enough, it'll enslave you.

But we don't have to feel *owned* by our doubts. Isn't it time we learn how to disengage a bit? To take a little doubt break. There are other things to do in life besides doubt all the time, right? Write someone a thank-you card. Take our spouse out for ice cream. Play catch with our son. Go bowling. Take a vacation. Watch a comedy. Laugh a little. Laugh a *lot*. And cry if we must. But we must refuse to become compulsive with our doubts. That's no way to live. We may exist that way, but I guarantee we won't live. We need a "doubt detox."

*Isn't it time we learn how to disengage
a bit? To take a little doubt break.*

Rest your mind a bit and give yourself permission to enjoy some of the simple things of life again. Don't worry about all your unanswered questions and trying to solve all of life's mysteries. There's more to life than that. Rather, give your doubts a bedtime and put them to sleep. Otherwise, they'll keep you up all the time. Shelve your doubts. Or even starve them. This isn't a cop-out; it's a respite. Later, when you feel mentally and emotionally ready, you can reengage. Don't worry, your doubts will be waiting for you, but this time in a *non*possessive way. Weaken the power of your doubts by refusing to overly obsess over them. It'll make a difference. Trust me.

Doubt Out Loud with Trusted Friends

Doubting out loud can feel risky. That's why it's important to share our doubts with trusted friends. Unfortunately, as we've briefly mentioned, the church hasn't done the best job handling doubters. This must change. Fast. Some believers express their doubts only to be met with agonizing *rejection*. Unfortunately, this causes many tormented doubters to leave the fold...never to return.

Remember Steve Jobs? Things don't have to be so either-or. I wonder how many disillusioned people leave their local church all because it appears that the world is where they find real acceptance. How sad that open arms and true grace are often found more among unbelievers than within the church. That's not the way it's supposed to be, Christians. Doubt—like fear, guilt, worry, depression, anger, stress, anxiety, and bitterness—needs a place to express itself. To leak. To be transparent. Authentic to the core.

> How sad that open arms and true
> grace are often found more among
> unbelievers than within the church.

I'm thankful that I've been the recipient of relational grace. I'm surrounded by church leaders who don't panic when I express doubt. Several years ago I was wrestling through a season of doubt, and I thought it was important to share with my elder team what was going on inside me. You know, in those deep spots. And their response was *heavenly*. Quite literally. They didn't freak out. They didn't ridicule me. Nor did they try to cheapen what was happening to me. No, these wise sages of Charlotte understood that doubt isn't a Christian problem. It's a human problem. And their response was so refreshing. "Bobby," they said, "everyone has doubts from time to time. You're not alone. We want to be there for you."

Talk about comforting. Their words were such a ministry to me. And as a result, my faith swelled up, soaring with renewed Christian hope. These men don't love me because I'm a Christian or because I hold to historic Christian doctrine. They love me because they love me. Period. Now *that's* a safe place where I can be real.

These men are smart enough to distinguish authentic doubt from antagonistic doubt. They knew I wasn't seeking to tear down Christianity. I wasn't seeking to dump biblical doctrine or to scrap systematic theology. I didn't have a bone to pick with the church. I just had an itch that needed a little community scratch. A place to doubt out loud. And their encouragement provided just what I needed to doubt toward faith. Isn't that what healthy community is supposed to do?

I've often wondered how different things could have been with my life had these guys thrown a fit, expressed disappointment, or felt theologically threatened by my questioning. Thank God they didn't.

> I hope you've got a few trusted friends
> with whom you can voice your doubts.
> Doubting in silence is torturous.

I hope you've got a few trusted friends with whom you can voice your doubts. Doubting in silence is torturous. There are moments I've thought, *Wouldn't it be great to belong to Doubters Anonymous.* "Hi, I'm Bobby and I'm a recovering doubter." (I say this tongue-in-cheek.) And then I remember that doubt doesn't have to be anonymous. As we saw in an earlier chapter, *Jesus can handle our doubts.* If that's the case, shouldn't His church be able to as well?

Know When to Doubt Your Doubts

"Jesus isn't God." These were the bold words my good friend expressed to me when I was a new believer. Sadly, I wasn't equipped enough in my faith to refute his claim. I had no theological well to draw from. I was simply bereft of an answer, and his statement drilled a small hole of doubt into me.

When we aren't equipped, we're more susceptible to doubt. I think that's why a lot of Christians don't evangelize. They don't know what to say, and they sure don't want to be caught off guard, exposed and answerless. That was me. I had no refutation. Looking back, this is one of those moments where I believe the Holy Spirit gave me an inward sense to doubt my doubt, an inclination that screamed, "Something doesn't smell right." While there are some things we need to doubt, there are some *doubts* we need to doubt as well.

> While there are some things we need to doubt,
> there are some *doubts* we need to doubt as well.

From now on, when doubt travels your direction, navigate your way out of doubt by habitually asking, "Do I need to doubt my doubt?" This allows you to shed unnecessary doubt. Not every thought you have is true. So question the ones that make you feel uncomfortable. And don't be afraid to be skeptical of your doubts.

Don't Be Surprised If the Cultural Wave of Doubt Grows Bigger

In her massive tome on doubt, atheist Jennifer Michael Hecht writes, "Where everyone seems to believe the same thing, doubt is calm."[4] While I don't agree with this statement entirely, there is some truth to it. Our culture is experiencing an epic shift in what people believe. We are shifting away from a once pro-Christian culture to a more anti-Christian one. And apart from a great awakening and spiritual revival, those of us who are Christians can expect to experience some persecution in the not-too-distant future.

The more our pro-Christian culture wanes, the more Christians in America must be willing to stand alone. This aloneness can spark doubt. Perhaps you have found yourself thinking, *What if I've got it wrong?* And the temptation may be to go with the masses. But truth doesn't necessarily exist with the masses. The truth was with Noah and his crew on the ark. And we know how that story unraveled for the masses.

....

We sort through the dizzying amount of contradictory beliefs, rejoicing that there is ample evidence for constructing a solid Christian faith.

....

I suspect this wave of doubt will only increase as our cultural beliefs clash against each other, cultivating an abundance of second-guessers. It would sure be easier if we didn't have so many competing beliefs. But that's not the world we live in. Only in heaven do they all agree on truth. In the meantime, we sort through the dizzying amount of contradictory beliefs, rejoicing that there is ample evidence for constructing a solid Christian faith.

Develop Your Ability to Discern

The New Testament Greek word *anakrino* is variously translated "discern," "examine," or "judge." It describes the ability to distinguish between right and wrong, between what's accurate and inaccurate. It's an inner GPS that guides us in the right direction. It's that faculty that allows us to determine what is true and what is false.

The great contemplative and sagacious author A.W. Tozer once wrote, "We need the gift of discernment again in our pulpits. It is not ability to predict that we need, but the anointed eye, the power of spiritual penetration and interpretation, the ability to appraise the religious scene as viewed from God's position, and to tell us what is actually going on."[5]

Tozer can proclaim these words from the shoulders of scriptural giants like Paul, who admonished the Thessalonians to "test everything; hold fast what is good."[6] John the apostle was another spiritual giant who stressed the need for discernment: "Beloved, do not believe every spirit, but test the spirits to see whether they are from God, for many false prophets have gone out into the world."[7] Paul cared so deeply about the church's ability to discern that it influenced the way he prayed: "And it is my prayer that your love may abound more and more, with knowledge and all *discernment*, so that you may approve what is excellent, and so be pure and blameless for the day of Christ."[8]

Given the importance of knowing what to doubt and what to believe, you might be asking, "But how do I develop my ability to discern?"

First, realize there is no such thing as discernment apart from wisdom. With that in mind, ask God to deepen your wisdom well. As James says, "If any of you lacks wisdom, let him ask God, who gives generously to all without reproach, and it will be given him."[9]

....

Ask God to deepen your wisdom well.

....

Second, get connected to a Bible-teaching church that has a high view of Scripture. It's hard to develop discernment in a church that exercises so little of it. Make sure you find a church that is passionate about truth and doesn't seek to bend the Bible to placate every cultural whim. Paul stressed to Timothy that God gave leaders to the church in order to equip their flocks.[10] And he even lists a key reason why they need to be equipped, "so that we may no longer be children, tossed to and fro by the waves and carried about by every wind of doctrine, by human cunning, by craftiness in deceitful schemes."[11] The apostle stresses that church leaders need to equip their flocks to separate truth from error. Wheat from chaff. Right from wrong.

Chase God's Heart

God's not throwing a hissy fit in heaven because you're carrying some doubt baggage. He's willing to engage you. Sometimes you just gotta pray through your doubts. The Bible says, "The Lord is near to all who call on him, to all who call on him *in truth*."[12] And He welcomes our questions, urging, "Come now, let us reason together, says the Lord."[13]

In the book of Jeremiah, we hear God's promise of hope to the survivors of the Babylonian captivity, "You will seek me and find me, when you seek me with all your *heart*. I will be found by you, declares the Lord."[14] The Jews went into captivity to begin with because they quit seeking God...exclusively. They no longer sought Him with all their heart. They were detached. Torn. And split in their affections. They went wayward instead of Godward. They adopted the manners and customs of the surrounding cultures, and in the process they lost sight of their relationship to God. This doubters club needed a strong dose of heart. And it's hard to find your way back to God while detached from your heart. Seeking God is a holistic discipline. It requires *all* of you. God's promise is on the line, "You will...find me." But there is also a condition: "When you seek me with all your heart."

> It's hard to find your way back to God
> while detached from your heart.

It's exhausting seeking a God who appears to be hiding out. Elusive. But we can be scripturally confident that He's here even if He doesn't seem near. Without question, the perceived absence of God's presence paves the way for more doubt.

But here's the remedy: Chase His heart with *all* your heart. Don't grow weary, confused, or exasperated. And whatever the case may be, refuse to detach your heart from your head on this God-quest. As you chase His heart, take comfort knowing that this isn't a dead-end search. It may be a long road, but it's not a dead end. So persevere. Don't quit. Don't even *think* about quitting.

Turn Your Doubt into a Song of Trust

The book of Psalms is a doubter's guide to transparent faith. In Psalm 88 the psalmist emotionally bleeds with doubt. From beginning to end the psalm is a cry of desperation. Psalm 74 is another psalm of brutal honesty filled with *why* questions and ending with a challenge for God to act...to do something. In Psalm 42 the psalmist is beat down, feeling downcast and forgotten. Yet he ends with a little pep talk to himself. Other psalms begin in deep desperation and end with an even deeper devotion. This is seen in Psalm 10 and Psalm 13.

....

The book of Psalms is a doubter's
guide to transparent faith.

....

What makes the latter psalm worth mentioning is the psalmist shifts from doubt to devotion and from sorrow to song. David, the writer of this psalm, wastes no time expressing himself in God's presence, asking repeatedly in the first two verses, "How long...how long...how long?" David is restless and weary, feeling forgotten and abandoned. He was longing for a little feedback from God. Yet, God's apparent disinterest cultivated in David a greater sense of earnestness. Despite God's detachment, David determines to doubt toward faith. He questions in the *forward* direction, even worshipping while he wonders. And you've gotta love it. Read it for yourself:

How long, O LORD? Will you forget me forever?
How long will you hide your face from me?
How long must I take counsel in my soul
and have sorrow in my heart all the day?
How long shall my enemy be exalted over me?
Consider and answer me, O LORD my God;
light up my eyes, lest I sleep the sleep of death,
lest my enemy say, "I have prevailed over him,"
lest my foes rejoice because I am shaken.
But I have trusted in your steadfast love;
my heart shall rejoice in your salvation.
I will sing to the LORD,
because he has dealt bountifully with me.[15]

In verse 5 we see that David chooses to trust, rejoice, and *sing*. Go figure.

Song has a way of merging our hearts with our heads. Music builds our hope artistically. When was the last time you musically expressed yourself through worship to God? Music has a way of waking up our hearts. Our hearts fall asleep when we are all head. And our head needs our heart to see clearly.

Sing your way out of doubt. The psalmists did.

Take a little time to clear your head by expressing your heart to God through song. Give it a shot. Sing your way out of doubt. The psalmists did.

Refresh Your Faith by Remembering God's Faithfulness

We just did a brief walk-through of Psalm 13. What I didn't point out is the final phrase of the psalm. In verse 6 David lists the reason for his singing, "because he *has* dealt bountifully with me." David found strength for the present by drawing it from the well of his past. In seasons of darkness, remember those moments when you clearly saw light on the path. In Psalm 77, after a little questioning, Asaph too reignites his faith with these words, "I will *remember* the deeds of the LORD; yes, I will *remember* your wonders of old."[16]

If you've read your Bible long enough, you're quite familiar with the oft-repeated word *remember*. God uses this word frequently because He knows our hearts and heads are prone to forget, that we all struggle with spiritual amnesia. God reminded Israel, saying, "You shall *remember* that you were a slave in the land of Egypt, and the LORD your God brought you out from there with a mighty hand and an outstretched arm."[17] The Israelites did forget that the Lord led them out of Egypt. And it didn't take long for their amnesia to kick in. When we struggle in the present, we need to remember our past God encounters.

> When we struggle in the present, we need to remember our past God encounters.

As shared, I have known the horror of intellectual doubt, but I have also had undeniable encounters with God. So when I'm racked with doubt, *I go back*. I mentally rewind to those faith encounters and remember that there is more to this relationship with God than getting my questions answered.

I remember the night He called me to ministry. How personal the invitation seemed.

I remember proposing to Heather through prayer as, on my knees, I asked the heavenly Father for her hand. *I remember* how I sensed His presence thickly descend upon me like the morning dew. He was there and it was quite otherworldly.

I remember praying with tears for guidance on whether I should attend Central Baptist Bible College in Conway, Arkansas. I had no idea how to pick a school. Heather just happened to be from Arkansas and told me about this little Bible college near her house. After imploring God to crystalize this decision, a few hours later I *remember* being at Saddleback Church at a Purpose-Driven Church Conference in Southern California when the guy sitting next to Heather picked up on her accent.

"Where are you from?" he asked.

"Arkansas," she said.

"I used to live in Arkansas in a little town called Conway," he said.

"I attended a little school you probably never heard of called Central Baptist College."

Heather was beside herself. She knew then that we were seeking God's direction. And when she told me, I knew I had my answer. Imagine that. A few hours earlier I was seeking God in my little black Ford Ranger pickup, and at a conference attended by two thousand people, God sat someone right next to Heather who had attended the very same college I was seeking God about. I *remember* that.

I remember how God's Spirit powerfully moved on day thirty-nine of my forty-day fast, ushering in a great movement on my college campus. Lives were changed. Souls were saved. And I stood in awe. I've never seen anything like it since.

I remember asking God to make Himself clear whether I was supposed to start a church in the Lake Norman area of North Carolina, the first suburbs north of Charlotte. It was a Thursday night and I had said, "I really need God to make this clear if we're supposed to start a church in Lake Norman." Heather and I were flying from Texas to North Carolina on Saturday, and on Friday I went to my Greek class at Dallas Theological Seminary. Partway through the lecture, a student sitting next to me, whom I hardly knew, said, "So, when do you graduate?"

(Greek class must have been pretty boring that day.)

I told him when and said, "I'm actually flying out to North Carolina tomorrow because we're looking at planting a church there."

"What part of North Carolina?" he asked.

"We're targeting the Lake Norman area." I'll never forget what he said next.

"No way. I actually went to Davidson College in the Lake Norman area. In fact, I was out jogging a week ago in my neighborhood, and when I finished the run, I went inside and said to my wife, 'Wouldn't it be cool if we could find a couple interested in planting a church in the Lake Norman area?'"

That person was Matt Hatfield. Today he's not only one of my best friends, but he sits on the elder team with me at Life Fellowship church in Davidson, North Carolina. Yeah, I *remember* that moment.

I **remember** *showing up in Charlotte the next day* and, in typical Bobby fashion, struggling again with doubt. I was like Gideon asking for one more sign. It was a big move, and I wanted to be sure that God was calling us there. I didn't want to plant a church in Lake Norman because it was beautiful or demographically growing. I wanted it to be God's idea.

So on Monday we were in Uptown Charlotte at a place that provides demographic information when a lady overheard us saying that Fellowship Bible Church of Little Rock was going to be planting a church and that we were considering the Lake Norman area.

"I know Don and Sally Meredith," she said. "They started Fellowship Bible Church of Little Rock, and they now live in the Lake Norman area. There's currently a group of people praying for a church like that to come our way."

I was stunned. Speechless. And convinced. I *remember* that. And from that point forward, we set our hearts on Lake Norman and have lived here since 2004. And go figure, the Merediths helped us start Life Fellowship and Melinda DeCusati, the lady we bumped into that day, served as a faithful member of our church for the first several years.

I **remember** *similar moments* and find great comfort looking through the rearview mirror. Remembering helps me see God's fingerprints all over my life.

Stoke the fires of your passion for Christ once
again by tracking His leadings through your life.

Let me encourage you to take a look through the rearview mirror of your faith walk and stoke the fires of your passion for Christ
once again by tracking His leadings through your life. Remember.

Choose to Believe Even When Things Seem Out of Control

Following Peter's courageous attempt to walk on water, which
ended with his near-drowning, Jesus said, "O you of little faith, why
did you *doubt*?"[18] I'm thinking, *Um, Jesus, because humans don't walk
on water.* And Peter at least tried, right?

But Jesus was probing for something deeper with Peter. Peter
doubted *Jesus*. That was the problem. As long as our eyes are on Jesus,
we can retain peace regardless of how turbulent the circumstances.
Even through a raging storm. As Isaiah writes, "You keep him in perfect peace whose mind is stayed on you, because he trusts in you."[19]

As long as our eyes are on Jesus, we
can retain peace regardless of how
turbulent the circumstances.

What's intriguing about this story is that Jesus actually believed
that as long as Peter's eyes were on Him, there was nothing to fear.
No need to doubt. Next time doubts plague you, revisit this simple
principle and refocus your eyes on Jesus. As long as Peter kept his
eyes on Jesus, he *was* walking on water. It's when he took his eyes off

of Jesus that his fears and doubts began to sink him. It's also when we begin to sink with doubt. And remember, as I once read somewhere, "Your hardest times often lead to the greatest moments of your life. *Keep the faith.* It will *all* be worth it in the end."

Times may be tough, but hang in there. You'll be glad you did.

Don't Just Study Your Beliefs—Live Them Out

Philosophers C. Stephen Evans and R. Zachary Manis write, "If we spent all our time critically reflecting on our faith, we would have no time to live out that faith. And religious faith is tested in part by the very process of living it out." [20] This sentiment is not meant to water down serious study. Evans and Manis stress that confident believers are willing to subject their views to counterviews and study the differences in their search for truth:

> If one is genuinely convinced that one's belief is true, one will not shrink from examining rival views. To the degree that one is certain and confident, one will welcome testing. A faith that evades critical questions is a faith that lacks confidence; a faith that is *not* truly assured it has found truth. Paradoxical as it may sound, confidence in one's convictions may make it possible to put those convictions to serious test. [21]

While these authors are adamant about diligent study, they know our faith is meant to be more than an academic exercise. It's meant to be *lived*. Even Jesus stressed this close connection between *doing* and *knowing,* saying, "If anyone's will is to *do* God's will, he will *know* whether the teaching is from God or whether I am speaking on my own authority." [22] Note the nexus. And get after it. When you're serving God and others, there's no time to obsess about yourself.

....

Perhaps you need a break from you. *Doubts have a way of drawing us inward.*

....

Perhaps you need a break from *you*. Doubts have a way of drawing us inward. So be cautious. Don't allow doubts to get you all coiled up in your brain. Get out there and live it.

Shift from Skeptical Doubt to Passionate Wonder

You've made a nice swap whenever you can exchange doubt for wonder. For those of you who have just a few questions that need a little massaging, you may be able to chase down all your doubts. For others, like myself, with a larger collection of doubts, you may need to embrace a little wonder. Whereas doubt can seem hopeless, wonder provides hope. Doubt is more cynical in nature and wonder is more optimistic. Doubt can despise mystery, but wonder celebrates it. And faith feeds off of it.

Thomas Aquinas, a thirteenth-century philosopher, was a master at thinking through people's doubts and objections and writing well-reasoned answers. After writing a mass of books, this Italian intellect had a mystical experience while celebrating mass on December 6, 1273, a few months before he died. This experience was so profound that he never picked up a pen to write again. He said to a friend, "I can write no more. All that I have written seems to me like so much straw compared to what I have seen and what has been revealed to me." If any skepticism remained in Aquinas, it all vanished after his encounter with God. If there was any doubt, it all turned to passionate wonder.

> When you get confused by God's awesomeness,
> remember to turn your doubts into wonder.

While we may not have a similar encounter, we can still learn to embrace a little wonder. When you get confused by God's awesomeness, remember to turn your doubts into wonder. Remember how the angel appeared to both Zechariah and Mary to inform them about the miracles they were to experience? For Zechariah, his wife would become pregnant in old age. And for Mary, though a virgin, she would give birth to the Messiah. Both experienced miracles. Each responded differently. Zechariah doubted toward unbelief; Mary wondered toward faith, even singing in wonder her matchless Magnificat.[23]

Consider a Spiritual Fast for a Spiritual Breakthrough

There is something about fasting that can lead to spiritual breakthroughs. I have seen God work amazingly in my life through both short and long fasts. Fasting is going without food (or something else, like technology) for a season so that we starve the flesh in order to strengthen our inner spirit. Life gets complicated, but by setting aside food in order to use that time to absorb God through prayer, reflection, journaling, and study, we can experience some great breakthroughs. Fasting can be both physically and spiritually refreshing.[24]

We've covered a lot of ground in this chapter. And as with any GPS, there are often several routes we can take to reach our destination. Why don't you take a little time to map out your own route based on some of the things we've learned together. Jot down a strategy and begin navigating your journey to confident Christianity.

Doubt Reflections

- *Weaken the power of your doubts by refusing to overly obsess over them.*

- *Discernment is the ability to know what to doubt and what to believe.*

- *Doubt is more cynical in nature and wonder is more optimistic.*

Questions for Further Thought and Discussion

1. What are some of the navigation points that resonated with you the most in this chapter?

2. Bobby distinguished between *doubt* and *wonder*. What are your thoughts on the relationship between these two words? Are you more of a doubter or a wonderer?

3. It's painful how forgetful we can be, isn't it? Why are we so spiritually forgetful and how can we learn to better *remember* God's past actions for us?

4. In this chapter the idea was expressed that we need to "doubt our doubts." How can discernment help Christians better know what to believe and what not to believe?

5. Jesus said, "Anyone who chooses to *do* the will of God will *know* whether my teaching comes from God." Elaborate on Jesus's words. What's the connection between *doing* and *knowing,* and do you have an

example of an aha moment of coming to know the truth by doing the truth?

6. Bobby said, "Seeking God is a holistic discipline. It requires *all* of you. God's promise is on the line, 'You will...find me.' But there is a condition: 'When you seek him with *all* your heart.' What does this really look like? And how can we know if we've truly sought Him with all our heart?

Chapter 9

FAITH DEFINED

"Ultimately, the problem with man is not the absence of evidence, it is the suppression of it."

Ravi Zacharias

"Faith is not a leap in the dark; it's the exact opposite. It's a commitment based on evidence."

John Lennox

It's no secret that our culture is rapidly changing, producing a cloud of confusion among believers. Once passionate, many believers are now experiencing a mass breakout of the doubts.

So far in this book we've seen that doubt is like having two minds, making us spiritually unstable. And we've discussed the ramifications as I described the acute agony of doubt. But we've also learned that Jesus can handle our doubts. We then discussed a number of different doubt triggers. Through this we familiarized ourselves with the various ways doubt disturbs our lives. Next we dug into the root of doubt and discussed Satan's role in attempting to dismantle us with doubts. Remember, he's not to be underestimated or overestimated but properly estimated. We also reviewed several facets of doubt, such as intellectual, emotional, spiritual, and evidential doubt. Finally, we talked about navigating our way *out* of doubt. And now, it's time to learn *how* to doubt toward *faith*.

> Faith is necessary if we're going to slay
> our doubts. Or at least reduce them.

In this chapter, we'll define faith. Faith is necessary if we're going to slay our doubts. Or at least reduce them. The good news is there's something about faith that thrills God. He loves it when we display faith in Him. So be encouraged. Our faith pleases Him immeasurably. Look at what the author of Hebrews says, "Without faith it is *impossible to please* him."[1] Let those words sink in for a moment. There is no pleasing God apart from faith. Notice the author doesn't say, "Without *certainty* it is impossible to please him."

It's no wonder that faith is an essential element every believer needs in order to please God. He knows we can't be know-it-alls. Only God knows everything. Remember, we are limited. Finite. And human. Our finitude cries out for faith, but our *fallenness* continues on in a futile search for certainty in every detail of life and faith. The other half of that same verse says, "for whoever would draw near to God must believe that he exists and that he rewards those who seek him."

So what can we glean from this verse?

First, part of drawing near to God means **believing** *that He exists.* Seems obvious, doesn't it? But how many of us have prayed empty prayers, given heartless lip service, and gone through the spiritual motions, all in a mindless and heartless pursuit? I have. And I'm betting you have too. That's called being a "functional atheist." Professing God but living as if He didn't exist.

Second, God **rewards** *those who seek Him with such faith.* Now that's exciting. Not only does our faith please God, but our faith is rewarded by Him.

Third, we have models to emulate. We find this in Hebrews 11, a chapter often referred to as "The Hall of Faith." We call it this because it's decorated with several examples of God-fearing individuals who exemplified extraordinary faith. In fact, this chapter gives us a long list of such examples. The author goes on to describe the faith of Noah, Abraham, Sarah, Isaac, Jacob, Joseph, Moses, the Israelites, Rahab, Gideon, Barak, Samson, Jephthah, David, Samuel, the prophets, faithful women, persecuted believers, and even martyrs.

Quite a who's who, isn't it?

As we read Hebrews 11, we notice these models of faith have two clear traits in common. First, though they're all flawed, each one nevertheless demonstrated great faith in God. Every flawed believer can have faith. And it's not the *amount* of faith that matters most, but the *nature* of it. Even our simple faith can be both effective and pleasing to God.[2] He can work with it—flaws and all. So, though this faith came from flawed individuals, it nevertheless was still faith. We can count on this. When we demonstrate faith in God—He is pleased. He *will* reward it. And He will even use it. But this begs the question, *What is faith?*

....

> Contrary to what you may have been
> taught, faith and reason aren't enemies.

....

Sometimes the best way to understand something is through understanding what it is *not*. Faith is not a free subscription to nonsense. It's not a flippant rejection of scientific facts. Contrary to what you may have been taught, faith and reason aren't enemies. They're allies. Friends. Cohorts. They work together. They're in sync. And Christians aren't the only ones who have faith. Everyone exercises some form of faith. Even the ardent atheist who thinks all his conclusions rest on solid proof still must exercise faith in some area of his life. A nullifidian, someone who supposedly has no faith, simply doesn't exist.

With this in mind, let's further unpack what faith is not in an attempt to grasp the nature of what faith is.

Faith Isn't Belief Without Evidence

This dichotomy of faith and reason is often promoted by antitheist professors, such as Steven Pinker, a Harvard cognitive psychologist, who declares, "Universities are about reason, pure and simple. Faith—believing something without good reasons to do so—has no place in anything but a religious institution, and our society has no shortage of these."[3]

What an unfortunate misunderstanding of the word *faith*. If faith truly is "believing something without good reasons to do so," then I'm not interested. And I trust you aren't either. Faith doesn't equal stupidity, naïveté, or even ignorance. Having faith in Christ isn't equivalent to a child's faith in the tooth fairy or the Easter bunny or Santa Claus. Apologists Ken Boa and Robert Bowman's book title nicely captures the difference: *Faith Has Its Reasons*. There is no reasonable evidence, beyond Mom and Dad, for a tooth fairy or the Easter bunny or Santa Claus.

Having faith in Christ isn't equivalent to
a child's faith in the tooth fairy or the
Easter bunny or Santa Claus.

During a lecture, atheist Richard Dawkins said, "Faith is the great cop-out, the great excuse to evade the need to think and evaluate the evidence. Faith is belief in spite of, even perhaps because of, the lack of evidence."[4] In *The God Delusion*, Dawkins pompously declares, "Faith is an evil precisely because it requires no justification and brooks no argument."[5]

Sam Harris, one of the most vociferous New Atheists, picks up on this rhetoric when he says, "Faith is generally nothing more than the permission religious people give one another to believe things strongly without evidence."[6] I'm not sure what kind of faith Harris has been paying attention to, but it's not the kind of faith the Bible (or I) advocates.

I will concede that the importance of the Christian mind has been made light of by some believers. I'm speaking of those whose mantra is "just believe" without engaging their intellect or reasonable thinking. But they do not represent all of Christianity.

There is a brand of Christianity that embraces the life of the mind with full fervor. These believers haven't forsaken reason for the comfort of intellectual laziness. They realize that faith isn't belief in the *absence* of reasonable evidence. Instead it's trust in the *presence* of reasonable evidence. The difference between the two is huge.

The New Atheist perspective I've cited here is pervasive in their circles. But it's nothing new. Mark Twain once quipped, "Faith is believing what you know ain't true." This type of discourse aims to belittle believers and make us feel silly, stupid, inept, and embarrassed. The ultimate goal is to silence us for our beliefs. And yet, many so-called intellectuals will deny reasonable evidence and do it in the name of doubting or skepticism.

> Many so-called intellectuals deny
> reasonable evidence and do it in the
> name of doubting or skepticism.

Consider the resurrection as a case in point. For the Christian, everything rises and falls on the resurrection of Jesus Christ. If He didn't rise from the dead, our faith is meaningless. Mythical. Apart from the empty tomb, our faith is empty.

In 1 Corinthians 15, Paul the apostle doesn't sound like some mystic hipster pushing for an ethereal, empty-minded experience when he speaks of the resurrection. No, in his great treatise on the resurrection, he adamantly states, "If Christ has not been raised, your faith is futile and you are still in your sins."[7] Read through this chapter and you can quickly see that Paul is building an *evidential* case for the resurrection. There is good *evidence* that Jesus really rose from the dead.[8]

After investigating the resurrection of Jesus Christ, atheist-turned-Christian Lee Strobel contended, "In the end, after I had thoroughly investigated the matter, I reached an unexpected conclusion: it would actually take *more faith* to maintain my atheism than to become a follower of Jesus."[9] What happened? Strobel found good *reasons* to believe.

But it appears that some just want to doubt regardless of the evidence. In his book *Jesus Among Other Gods,* Ravi Zacharias writes:

> I am convinced that there are tens of thousands of students turned out of our universities whose minds have been trained to disbelieve in God, any contrary

argument or evidence notwithstanding. The father of modern rationalism is the French philosopher Rene Descartes. His dictum—"I think, therefore I am"—resonates in the halls of philosophy. From that fundamentally rationalistic approach to existence, skeptics have extrapolated their own dictum—"I doubt, therefore I am an intellectual." For many, such doubting actually follows a particular intellectual, rather than squarely facing the questions of the intellect. [10]

Christians, like atheists, believe in evidence. And I'm not talking about some painfully thin shred of tainted evidence either. No, both groups claim evidence to support their belief systems. And both place their *faith* in their findings. The question is, who's right? Who has the most convincing and credible evidence?

The ardent atheist places his faith in the evidence he believes is provided through materialism, while the ardent Christian places his faith in the evidence he believes is provided through both materialism and supernaturalism. Christians don't have faith without evidence. And atheists don't have evidence without faith. Both Christians and atheists have both faith *and* evidence.

....

I agree with those who say, "I don't have
enough faith to be an atheist."

....

I agree with those who say, "I don't have enough faith to be an atheist." One difference between the atheist and the Christian is that the atheist has two blind spots. He doesn't think Christians have evidence and he doesn't think *he* has faith. It's hard to see clearly when you're doubly blind. It's also hard to follow the directions of a blind man. In the meantime, I'll keep my faith linked with those who have sight.

Faith Isn't a Crutch for the Naïve

Christians have a rich legacy of robust thinkers who passionately believed in God. Christianity isn't a crutch for naïve and weak-minded thinkers. Consider such highbrowed believers as Nicolaus Copernicus, Sir Francis Bacon, Johannes Kepler, Galileo Galilei, Blaise Pascal, Isaac Newton, Robert Boyle, and Michael Faraday. These thinkers weren't imbeciles. Or consider the robust theologians and philosophers, such as Augustine, Thomas Aquinas, Martin Luther, John Calvin, Jonathan Edwards, Søren Kierkegaard, Dietrich Bonhoeffer, G.K. Chesterton, and C.S. Lewis. No intellectual losers in this list.

Christian intellectuals aren't merely a relic of the past; erudite thinkers still walk among us today. Names such as Alvin Plantinga, Richard Swinburne, William Lane Craig, N.T. Wright, Alister McGrath, John Lennox, and many more grace the halls of academe with brilliant minds. When I consider this list, I think, *Not too shabby*. And that's just scratching the surface.

> It is dishonest to characterize the community
> of faith as being comprised only of
> simpleminded people. We have some
> heavyweight contenders in our corner.

However, I'm not implying that Christianity is only for the bright minded or the intellectual elite. I'm simply showing that it is dishonest to characterize the community of faith as being comprised only of simpleminded people. We have some heavyweight contenders in our corner. The scholars I've listed are some of the finest thinkers in human history. And for that, I rejoice. When I get in an intellectual snag, I find great comfort in knowing that there are people far smarter than I who still bow their knee to the great I AM. Maybe, just maybe, that is part of the secret to their genius.[11]

Faith Doesn't Mean You'll Get All Your Questions Answered

Philosopher William Lane Craig says, "The secret to dealing with doubt in the Christian life is not to resolve all of one's doubts. One will always have unanswered questions. Rather, the secret is learning to live victoriously with one's unanswered questions."[12] And this too is achieved by faith. Regardless of a person's belief, life will still be full of unanswered questions. While Christianity provides ample evidence, it doesn't provide exhaustive evidence. However, faith in the evidence of what we can know increases our faith in what we can't know.

> Faith in the evidence of what we can know increases our faith in what we can't know.

For example, while we don't have extrabiblical evidence for *everything* in the Old Testament, we do have the affirmation of Jesus about the Old Testament. But how does this help? We can reason as follows. If Jesus really rose from the dead, and if He believed in the Old Testament Scriptures, then based on His testimony we can confidently believe too. Granted, some areas may seem hard to grasp, but based on our grasp of Jesus, we can by faith grasp the rest without being restless.

Many doubters panic when they cross the threshold into the

unknown. But learning to replace panic with serenity in the valleys of the unknown will go a long way to improving our faith journey.

Faith Isn't Empty-Headedness

This is important. The Cambridge dictionary defines faith as "a high degree of trust or confidence in something or someone."[13] In the Bible, we see examples of faith that vary in degree from low to high.[14] Nineteenth-century American poet Emily Dickinson once wrote, "We both believe, and disbelieve a hundred times an Hour, which keeps Believing nimble."[15]

God obviously desires our degree of faith to be on the high side. He wants us to have complete confidence in Him. To trust Him. Nevertheless, we are fickle little creatures. Notice, the Cambridge dictionary didn't define faith as a shot in the dark. Rather, it is having "trust or confidence in something or someone."

In their book *In Search of Confident Faith*, J.P. Moreland and Klaus Issler define faith as "trusting what we have reason to believe is true."[16] According to that definition, Dawkins, Harris, and the like aren't being honest with what a believer believes about faith. Moreland and Issler further write, "Faith is only as good as the nature of its object."[17] They heartily recognize the confusion today around the word *faith* and even suggest replacing *faith* with *confidence* in our discussions with others.[18] Think about it. Confidence is placed in something or someone for a good reason. There's evidence to give us confidence. It's the same with trust. We trust in something or someone because we believe the object of our trust is reliable. So it turns out that faith isn't empty-headed after all.

....

"Faith is only as good as the nature of its object."

....

But what does faith look like? Consider the baseball coach who has faith in his left-handed relief pitcher, or the farmer who has faith that his crops will produce a harvest, or the husband who has faith that his wife will always be faithful to him. The coach, the farmer, and the husband all have one thing in common. They each have confidence.

When a coach says he has faith in his pitcher, he's really saying, "I'm confident he will get the job done." When the farmer says he has faith that his crops will produce a harvest, he's really saying, "I'm confident in the laws of the harvest." And when a husband says he has faith that his wife will be faithful, he's really saying, "I trust my bride." In each case, there is good reason to have faith, to show trust, and to exercise confidence. The coach knows the caliber of his pitcher, the farmer believes you reap what you sow, and the husband has complete trust in the character of his wife.

This is far from blind faith gutted of reasonable evidence. Many people's mocking view of faith would have you believe that faith is really the baseball coach saying, "I've got great faith that my dog Constance will strike out the side." Or the farmer saying, "I can't wait to see what kind of harvest I'll get from the recently poured concrete." Or the husband saying, "I know my wife has had thirty affairs, but this time it'll be different. I promise." Such examples of "faith" are devoid of any reason for trust.

Confidence entails reason for confidence. And so does faith because faith is confidence. The author of Hebrews even gives us a definition of faith, writing, "Now faith is the *assurance* of things hoped for, the *conviction* of things not seen."[19] Both the assurance and conviction are based on evidence, and that is what produces a solid hope.[20]

With these thoughts in mind, we must remember that while

evidence is important, it's not enough. We must ultimately commit ourselves to God.

Now *that's* faith.

Doubt Reflections

- *Next time you doubt, remember there's something about faith that thrills God.*

- *Faith doesn't equal stupidity, naïveté, or even ignorance.*

- *If you're going to slay your doubts, or at least reduce them, biblical faith will be required.*

Questions for Further Thought and Discussion

1. Bobby said, "There's something about faith that thrills God. He *loves* it when you display faith *in* Him." Why is this so important for Christians to grasp?

2. The next time an atheist says to you something like, "Faith is for the empty-headed," or "Faith is what people turn to when they have no evidence," how will you respond?

3. How does understanding the word *faith* as confidence help crystalize the word for you?

4. Moreland and Issler suggest using the word *confidence* instead of *faith* when conversing with nonbelievers. Do you agree or disagree with this strategy?

5. In this chapter, Bobby gave quite the list of intellectual

Christians from both our present and the past. Do you find that comforting? If so, why?

6. Watch this brief interview Bobby did on *The One Minute Apologist* where he asks Hank Hanegraaff, "What Is a Good Biblical Definition of Faith?" (www. youtube.com/watch?v=Le0yZDykkmg). Then share your thoughts and reactions to what was said.

Chapter 10

TOWARD FAITH

*"Faith is not belief without proof but trust
without reservations—trust in a God who
has shown himself worthy of that trust."*

ALISTER MCGRATH

*"I best learn about my own need for faith during its absence.
God's invisibility guarantees I will experience times of doubt."*

PHILIP YANCEY

In discussing matters of faith, we have to recognize that not all of our questions will be answered, at least not in this lifetime. You may wonder, "So what about mystery? Isn't faith just a category for coping with things we don't fully understand?"

In his beloved book *Orthodoxy,* G.K. Chesterton writes concerning mystery, "Mysticism keeps men sane. As long as you have mystery you have health; when you destroy mystery you create morbidity...The morbid logician seeks to make everything lucid, and succeeds in making everything mysterious. The mystic allows one thing to be mysterious, and everything else becomes lucid."[1]

The moral of the story is this: One sure way to lose your sanity is to try to make sense of everything. Ours is a world *beyond* full comprehension. And for that, there is such a thing as mystery. Christianity has its fair share of mysteries, but as I once heard it put, "Mystery is not the absence of meaning but the presence of more meaning than we can comprehend."

> One sure way to lose your sanity is to
> try to make sense of everything.

While many doubts appear to be forever draped in mystery, believers are able to trust God with life's unknowns because we have deemed God trustworthy with so much that *can* be known. It is what we already know about God as believers that enables us to trust Him with the great unknowns. The confidence that we have in the evidence He has provided gives us confidence to trust Him with what He hasn't provided.

He has given us knowledge of Himself, how the world came into being, how we can be rescued from sin's curse, and how to know Him in a personal way. Surely, if He has revealed all of this to us, we can trust Him with the mysteries we don't yet know or understand. And besides, mystery is necessary for wonder and wonder is good for the imagination. In an age of reason, were all the codes to be unlocked, life would lose its sense of wonder, becoming boring, bland, and banal. God is an infinitely awesome God, and it can't hurt the believer to allow life's mystery to create a little awe and wonder.

> God is infinitely awesome, and it can't
> hurt the believer to allow life's mystery
> to create a little awe and wonder.

The Role of Faith in the Believer's Life

We've seen that faith isn't belief without evidence, nor is it a crutch for the naïve, nor is faith a form of empty-headedness. Rather, faith is confident trust in reliable evidence. Yet because of all the evidence provided, faith can also help us in the mystery department. Beyond this, Scripture reveals even more about faith. In fact, the Bible is replete with verses about the role of faith in the believer's life. Here are some examples:

We are to live by faith. Paul writes to the Romans, "The righteous shall live by faith."[2] Paul uses this same phrase in his letter to the Galatians.[3] And the author of Hebrews, tuned to the same station, aligns with Paul.[4] In all three instances, the New Testament writers are quoting from the Old Testament prophet Habakkuk.[5]

Faith is a lifestyle. An attitude of dependence. It's how we live, moment by moment. Depending on God. Trusting in Him. And keeping our confidence firmly rooted in Him through the highs and lows of life. This is closely related to Paul's admonition to the Corinthians when he said, "For we walk by faith, not by sight."[6] We walk by faith by living with a confident trust in God. We focus on what is ultimate and refuse to let everyday trials knock us out of spiritual alignment with God. We walk straight. Therefore, we walk by faith, not by sight.

We are saved by grace through faith. In Paul's epistle to the

Ephesians, he writes, "For by grace you have been saved *through faith*."[7] We experience new life in Christ when God's grace meets us with saving faith.

Our faith is strengthened as we give glory to God. This is what happened to Abraham. Far from decreasing, Abraham's faith increased as he confidently trusted in God's promise to provide an heir through whom all nations would be blessed. "No unbelief made him waver concerning the promise of God, but *he grew strong in his faith* as he *gave glory* to God, fully convinced that God was able to do what he promised."[8]

I'm happy to say that our doubts are not the only thing that can grow. Our faith can too.[9] And doubts shrink when our faith is stretched. If you want to decrease your doubt, increase your faith. Doubts are erased as faith expands. Doubts deflate in the presence of an enlarged faith. So grow your faith. Stretch it. Increase it. Expand it by confidently trusting in God's Word and giving Him glory where glory is due.

> Doubts deflate in the presence of an enlarged faith. So grow your faith. Stretch it. Increase it.

Christ is the object of our saving faith. "Faith comes from hearing, and hearing through the word of Christ."[10] By hearing the gospel through the ears of saving faith, we're able to tower above the doubts that prevent us from coming to Christ.

God can use our faith to comfort others. Such was the case as Timothy brought encouraging news about the Thessalonians' faith, and this good news inspired Paul and his companions: "But now that Timothy has come to us from you, and has brought us the good news of your faith and love and reported that you always remember us kindly and long to see us, as we long to see you—for this reason, brothers, in all our distress and affliction we have been comforted about you through your faith."[11] When our faith is in despair, we can be thankful that there's always someone out there whose faith is on display.

Faith can shield us from the evil one's attacks. To the Ephesians Paul writes, "In all circumstances take up the shield of faith, with which you can extinguish *all* the flaming darts of the evil one."[12] If we're going to survive this thing called spiritual warfare, then we must carry the shield of faith. The evil one will aim his doubt darts our way, and the shield of confident faith will enable us to smash doubt.

We are to follow spiritual leaders who model faith. The author of Hebrews writes, "Remember your leaders, those who spoke to you the word of God. Consider the outcome of their way of life, and imitate their faith."[13] What an exhortation.

Our faith needs to be tested so that we can be properly sanctified. James says, "For you know that the testing of your faith produces steadfastness. And let steadfastness have its full effect, that you may be perfect and complete, lacking in nothing."[14]

Prayer must be accompanied with faith. James also says, "But let him ask in faith, *with no doubting,* for the one who doubts is like a wave of the sea that is driven and tossed by the wind. For that person must not suppose that he will receive anything from the Lord; he is a double-minded man, unstable in all his ways."[15]

The quality of our faith will be tested. "In this you rejoice, though now for a little while, if necessary, you have been grieved by various trials, so that the tested genuineness of your faith—more precious than gold that perishes though it is tested by fire—may be found to result in praise and glory and honor at the revelation of Jesus Christ. Though you have not seen him, you love him. Though you do not now see him, you believe in him and rejoice with joy that is inexpressible and filled with glory, obtaining the outcome of your faith, the salvation of your souls."[16]

Our faith in Jesus Christ ultimately helps us to overcome the world. "For everyone who has been born of God overcomes the world. And this is the victory that has overcome the world—our faith. Who is it that overcomes the world except the one who believes that Jesus is the Son of God?"[17] It's this very faith in Jesus Christ that ultimately triumphs.

Christians are to contend for the faith in the midst of false teaching. Jude urges believers "to contend for the faith that was once for all delivered to the saints. For certain people have crept in unnoticed who long ago were designated for this condemnation, ungodly people, who pervert the grace of our God into sensuality and deny our only Master and Lord, Jesus Christ."[18]

When Jesus returns again, He will be looking for faith. In fact, faith is so important that Jesus even asks, "When the Son of man comes, will he find faith on earth?"[19] Will He find faith in you? And in me? I sure hope so.

> It's hard to confront our doubts if we don't
> know what the Bible has to say about faith.

The verses above depict the importance of faith in the believer's life. Let me encourage you to come back to those verses and prayerfully consider them more fully. It's hard to confront our doubts if we don't know what the Bible has to say about faith. In fact, faith is what enables us to confront our doubts.

Philip Yancey writes in his book *Reaching for the Invisible God,* "Those who honestly confront their doubts often find themselves growing into a faith that transcends doubts."[20] The good news is that doubt can truly be the pathway toward a *deeper* faith. It's only through relentless searching, questioning, examining, and probing that we can swim farther into the deep end of our religious belief. While doubt can be destructive to our faith, it turns out that doubt can have a beneficial effect as well—when doubt meets faith. Faith can take us out of the quicksand of doubt. The Lord said through the prophet Isaiah, "If you are not firm in faith, you will not be firm at all." [21]

It's only through relentless searching, questioning, examining, and probing that we can swim farther into the deep end of our religious belief.

Doubt will make us restless. Faith will make us restful. Doubt will cause us to be in two minds. Faith will place us in one mind. Doubt will sap our strength; faith will saturate us with strength. Doubt will lead to fear, worry, anger, depression, and more, whereas faith will lead to trust, serenity, peace, and hope. Faith puts our spiritual sight in proper perspective. Paul put it like this, "For now we see in a mirror dimly, but then face to face. Now I know in part; then I shall know fully, even as I have been fully known." [22] You could almost hear Paul saying, "For now we've got enough evidence to proceed forward by faith, but there's coming a day when mystery will turn to certainty."

The Self-Authenticating Witness of the Holy Spirit

The self-authenticating witness of the Holy Spirit plays a key role in confirming the faith of a believer, especially a doubting believer. Paul writes, "The Spirit himself bears witness with our spirit that we are children of God."[23] The internal witness of the Holy Spirit provides assurance to the legitimacy of the Christian faith. The dependent believer in Jesus knows that the Holy Spirit plays a crucial role in assuaging his doubts, assuring him of the truthfulness of Christianity even in the absence of evidence.

> The dependent believer in Jesus knows that the Holy Spirit plays a crucial role in assuaging his doubts.

Alvin Plantinga, arguably the greatest living Christian philosopher, contends that a Christian is still warranted to hold his belief whether he can summon the evidence to support it or not. Plantinga shares the winsome illustration of someone who is accused of a crime, and in spite of all the evidence stacked against him, this person is truly innocent. Plantinga contends that person is justified to believe in his innocence even though he appears to be guilty. Similarly, the Christian may be at a loss for words and unable to provide an answer to defeat someone's objections to Christianity, yet this doesn't mean the believer should abandon his belief. Rather, the believer is justified to hold fast to his faith.

This isn't wishful thinking. In the same way that we are justified in believing in a real external world, or in other minds, or in a real past, or in memories without evidence, our belief in God is also justified. And better yet, on top of this assurance the Christian is extra-warranted by the ample evidences at his disposal. So take heart. William Lane Craig, using Plantinga's line of reasoning, applies this warrant for belief to the Holy Spirit as a means of assurance in Christian belief.[24]

As we've seen, doubt can be debilitating. It can hang over us like a dark cloud that appears permanently fixed. It can electrocute our emotions rendering us with a tenuous faith. This doubt can feel like an incurable disease that wears us down in utter hopelessness.

A confident belief in the work of the Holy Spirit can allay such *weltschmerz*.[25] During a season of doubt, a nice dose of Ephesians 1:13-14 can be spiritually medicinal, as it reminds us, "In him you also, when you heard the word of truth, the gospel of your salvation, and believed in him, were sealed with the promised Holy Spirit, who is the guarantee of our inheritance until we acquire possession of it, to the praise of his glory."

If there's one thing we can be sure of, it's this. God doesn't want us to be Christian agnostics. John the apostle wrote an entire epistle to provide such confidence of belief: "I write these things to you who believe in the name of the Son of God that you may *know* that you have eternal life."[26] John stressed the word *believe* in his writing. In doing so, he was essentially saying, "Don't disbelieve. Rather believe. Continue to doubt toward faith." As Danish philosopher Søren Kierkegaard once said, "Faith is a project for a lifetime."

Train Your Way Out of Doubt

If you're a doubt addict, then you'll need to train your way out of your doubts. Here's what I mean. We've all heard the illustration about viewing a glass filled to the halfway mark as being either half-full or half-empty. That's sort of like our walk with God. We can dwell on and obsess over criticisms of Christianity, but viewing our faith through such a half-empty lens is a guaranteed way to overwhelm ourselves with doubt. Or we can train ourselves to see the glass as half-full, realizing that there are credible answers to our curious questions. For me, I made a *decision* to see the glass half-full. And it's made all the difference.

> If you're a doubt addict, then you'll need
> to train your way out of your doubts.

So whenever your next doubt comes your way, give the Scriptures the benefit of the doubt lest you treat the Bible forever as guilty until proven innocent. Train your way into a deeper faith by seeing the glass as half-full.[27] Follow the strategy Paul once shared, "We destroy arguments and every lofty opinion raised against the knowledge of God, and take every thought captive to obey Christ."[28]

A Tale of Two Doubters

During the mid-twentieth century, two highly gifted evangelists were mightily used by God. They were great friends with promising futures. But there was one problem—both were being pounded by a faith crisis. Both were tangled up with doubt. And when all was said and done, one doubted toward faith, while the other doubted toward unbelief. One's faith crisis crumbled his Christianity, while the other person's faith crisis cemented his belief in Christianity.

Who are these two figures from yesteryear? The first doubter, Charles Templeton, would never return to his once-professed faith. In 1996 he published *Farewell to God*, one of the saddest book titles in human history. Five years later, Templeton would slip into a Christless eternity, dying as an apostate. Tragic.

The year following Templeton's release of *Farewell to God*, the second doubter, Billy Graham, published his autobiography, *Just As I Am*. In it he unveils his battle with doubt in agonizing detail. Recalling his dark night of the soul, Graham wrote, "My faith is under siege."[29] His account of that night and the victory that ensued are worth reading:

As that night wore on, my heart became heavily burdened. Could I trust the Bible?…If I *could not* trust the Bible, I could not go on…I would have to leave pulpit evangelism. I was only thirty years of age. It was not too late to become a dairy farmer. But that night I believed with all my heart that the God who had saved my soul would never let go of me.

I got up and took a walk. The moon was out. The shadows were long in the San Bernardino Mountains surrounding the retreat center. Dropping to my knees there in the woods, I opened the Bible at random on a tree stump in front of me. I could not read it in the shadowy moonlight, so I had no idea what text lay before me…

The exact wording of my prayer is beyond recall, but it must have echoed my thoughts: "O God. There are many things in this book I do not understand. There are many problems with it for which I have no solution. There are many seeming contradictions. There are some areas in it that do not seem to correlate with modern science. I can't answer some of the philosophical and psychological questions…"

I was trying to be on the level with God, but something remained unspoken. At last the Holy Spirit freed me to say it. "Father, I am going to accept this as Thy Word— by *faith*. I'm going to allow faith to go beyond my intellectual questions and doubts, and I will believe this to be Your inspired Word."

When I got up from my knees at Forest Home that August night, my eyes stung with tears. I sensed the presence and power of God as I had not sensed it in months. Not all my questions were answered, but a major bridge had been crossed. In my heart and mind, I knew a spiritual battle in my soul had been fought and won.[30]

Far from committing intellectual suicide that night, Billy Graham properly understood that no matter how hard he studied, he'd never comprehend everything. He was content to live with mystery and follow Christ faithfully.

....

> Billy Graham was content to live with
> mystery and follow Christ faithfully.

....

Graham descended that mountain a different man. The very next month brought his greatest opportunity to date. In 1949, he led an extended crusade in Los Angeles that was so powerfully used by the Lord that when it ended, Graham was a nationally acclaimed evangelist. *Newsweek* one year later referred to him as "America's Greatest Living Evangelist." And the rest is history.

From where I write, that dairy farmer born in Charlotte lives only two hours away. Well into his nineties, he's breathing in the air of faith from Black Mountain, sitting satisfied and thankful that he doubted toward faith.

Every believer must come to grips with their doubts. During a conversation about doubt, Dennis Rainey, the president of Family Life, shared with me from memory a statement that Tom Skinner, the former chaplain of the Washington Redskins, shared with him many years ago. Skinner said, "I spent a long time trying to come to grips with my doubts, when suddenly I realized that I had better come to grips with what I believe. I have since moved from the agony of questions that I cannot answer to the reality of answers that I cannot escape...and it's a great relief."

....

Every believer must come to
grips with their doubts.

....

What a statement. Words so powerful that Dennis quoted them to me with emphasis I think three times in a row. As if to say, "Bobby, chew on these words." And chew I did. Like Graham, Skinner doubted toward faith. And his faith wasn't birthed out of an absence of knowledge but out of the evidence of what he *could* know.

As we wrap up, here's the good news. You too can experience relief from your doubts. Do you believe that? There's great relief waiting for you. Even today. But you've got a decision to make. You've got to come to grips with your doubts. So, I beg you, don't lose hope. You've got this thing. Get a grip right now and, like Billy Graham and Tom Skinner, doubt *toward* faith.

Take the "Doubting Toward Faith" Fourfold Challenge

1. Form a small group to discuss the questions at the end of each chapter.

2. Ask your doubting friends or family to read this book and discuss it with them.

3. Map out a strategy with your pastoral team that will help your church to doubt toward faith.

4. Begin utilizing Bobby's website at www.oneminuteapologist.com to help you with the questions that seek to trip up your faith. Begin watching the hundreds of videos provided so that you can provide credible answers to curious questions.

Doubt Reflections

- *Doubts shrink when our faith is stretched.*

- *Doubt will make you restless. Faith will make you restful.*

- *"When the Son of man comes will he find faith on earth?"—Jesus*

Questions for Further Thought and Discussion

1. Thinking through the book as a whole, what are your biggest takeaways?

2. Of the many biblical examples of faith, which ones stood out to you the most?

3. What would you say to someone who said, "Even Mormons claim assurance of faith due to the witness of the Holy Spirit"? For further help, read the link Bobby provided to access William Lane Craig's insights on the witness of the Holy Spirit.

4. Bobby said, "If you're a doubt addict, then you'll need to train your way out of your doubts." What are some ways Christians can train their way out of doubt?

5. Charles Templeton and Billy Graham each had a decision to make regarding their doubts. How can the church do a better job helping doubters not to say "farewell to God"?

6. At the end of this chapter Bobby offered up a fourfold challenge. Will you take it?

TWO EXTRA TIPS FOR NAVIGATING DOUBT

Take Good Physical Care of Yourself

Sometimes in the church we can fail to mention the simple importance of just taking good physical care of ourselves. Obviously, our physical health is just one piece of the puzzle, but we can't neglect the importance of a healthy lifestyle. For example, if our caffeine intake is over the top, it can take our emotions that are impacted by doubt for an unpleasant ride. The result can be panic and anxiety and mental fidgeting. Besides caffeine, too much sugar, alcohol, nicotine, and medication, and a lack of exercise and sleep can all contribute to our sense of stuck*ness*. All of this can serve to heighten and magnify our doubts.

So take good care of yourself. When you're trying to get to the bottom of your doubts, it's critical to consider all the things that could unnecessarily interfere with your sanity. It's worth the peace of mind that your troubleshooting is thorough. I trust you agree.

Consider Seeking Trusted Professional Help

At times, life can wear some people out so much that they no longer desire to live. It can get that desperate. While I hope that's not you, if it is, please be sure to visit a trusted Christian counselor. It could be that hormonal issues or certain chemically related imbalances are disorienting your emotional well-being and thought processes.

We are an overly medicated culture, but as a *last resort,* a wise counselor can assess whether you need further evaluation and treatment. However, be discerning about this. I've never used medication to assuage my doubts and anxieties, but at times it was tempting. Medications come with lots of side effects, yet sometimes the battle seems so overwhelming that we'll swap out one set of consequences for another set if it means finding reprieve.

I realize I'm on controversial turf here. But some people will slip into such a desperate state that I'd rather advise them to get help before they perhaps do something drastic to themselves or others. This isn't caving in. It's common sense.

NOTES

Chapter 1: A Crisis of Doubt

1. Os Guinness, *Renaissance* (Downers Grove, IL: InterVarsity Press, 2014), 25.

2. Philosopher James K.A. Smith describes *fragilization* as follows, "In the face of different options, where people who lead 'normal' lives do not share my faith (and perhaps believe something different), my own faith commitment becomes fragile—put into question, dubitable." *How (Not) to Be Secular* (Grand Rapids, MI: Wm. B. Eerdmans, 2014), 141.

3. Lillian Kwon, "Survey: High School Seniors 'Graduating from God,'" *The Christian Post*, August 10, 2006.

4. You'll often find elements of truth in different belief systems, and where that's the case, we can remember Augustine's dictum, "All truth is God's truth."

5. William Lane Craig, *Hard Questions, Real Answers* (Wheaton, IL: Crossway, 2003), 33-34, emphasis in the original.

6. See Matthew 14:31; 21:21; 28:17; Mark 11:23; Luke 24:38; Romans 14:23; James 1:6-8; and Jude 22.

7. Gary Habermas, *The Thomas Factor* (Nashville, TN: Broadman and Holman, 1999), 4-5, emphasis added.

8. Os Guinness, *In Two Minds* (Downers Grove, IL: InterVarsity Press, 1976).

9. Vincent Bugliosi, "Why Do I Doubt Both the Atheists and the Theists?" (2011), *Religious Tolerance.org*, www.religioustolerance.org/bugliosi01.htm.

10. Matthew 16:18, emphasis added.

Chapter 2: A Splinter in the Mind

1. Mother Teresa, *Mother Teresa: Come Be My Light: The Private Writings of the Saint of Calcutta*, ed. Brian Kolodiejchuk (New York: Doubleday Religion, 2007), 169-70.

2. Jude 22.

3. I. John Hesselink, *Calvin's First Catechism: A Commentary* (Louisville, KY: Westminster John Knox Press, 1997), 103.

4. C.H. Spurgeon, "The Desire of the Soul in Spiritual Darkness," *The Spurgeon Archive*, June 24, 1855, www.spurgeon.org/sermons/0031.htm.

5. C.S. Lewis, *Mere Christianity* (New York: HarperCollins, 2001), 140.

6. Karl Barth, *Evangelical Theology: An Introduction* (Grand Rapids, MI: Wm. B. Eerdmans, 1979), 131.

7. Francis Schaeffer, Preface to *True Spirituality* (Wheaton, IL: Tyndale House, 1972).

8. Billy Graham, "Answers," Billy Graham Evangelistic Association, November 18, 2004, http://billygraham.org/answer/does-doubt-come-from-the-devil-or-do-we-have-doubts-because-of-something-thats-wrong-in-our-hearts/.

9. Genesis 18:12.

10. Habakkuk 1:3.

11. Luke 1:8-18.

12. Matthew 11:3.

13. John 20:25.

14. Matthew 28:17, emphasis added.

15. Matthew 27:46.

16. C. Stephen Evans & R. Zachary Manis, *Philosophy of Religion* (Downers Grove, IL: InterVarsity Press, 2009), 208.

17. Nihilism is the belief that life is utterly meaningless.

18. Visit www.oneminuteapologist.com or www.bobbyconwayonline.com.

19. Andrew Hoffecker, "Doubt and the Apologist," *Tabletalk*, Ligonier Ministries, www.ligonier.org/learn/articles/doubt-and-the-apologist/.

20. Habakkuk 2:4.

21. Mother Teresa, *Mother Teresa: Come Be My Light*, 167.

Chapter 3: Jesus Can Handle Your Doubts

1. Walter Isaacson, *Steve Jobs* (New York: Simon & Schuster, 2011), 14-15.

2. Kara Powell, "Steve Jobs, Back to School, and Why Doubt Belongs in Your Youth Group Curriculum," *Christianity Today*, September 2012, www.christianitytoday.com/women/2012/september/steve-jobs-back-to-school-and-why-doubt-belongs-in-your.html?start=2.

3. Philip Yancey, "Faith and Doubt," www.philipyancey.com/q-and-a-topics/faith-and-doubt.

4. John 3:30.

5. Matthew 3:2.

6. John 1:29.

7. See Matthew 2:16.

8. Matthew 11:2.

9. Matthew 11:4-5.

10. See Isaiah 35:5-6; 61:1.

11. Matthew 11:7-11.

12. 1 Timothy 2:5; Hebrews 4:14-16.

13. Jeremiah 29:13, emphasis added.

14. James 1:5-6.

15. J. Warner Wallace, "How Jesus Responded to Doubt," http://coldcasechristianity.com/2013/how-jesus-responded-to-doubt/.

16. Matthew 11:7.

17. Matthew 11:11, emphasis added.

18. Gary Habermas, *The Thomas Factor* (Nashville, TN: Broadman & Holman Publishing, 1999), 29.

19. Powell, "Steve Jobs, Back to School, and Why Doubt Belongs in Your Youth Group Curriculum."

Chapter 4: Doubt Triggers: Part 1

1. See William Lane Craig, *Reasonable Faith* (Wheaton, IL: Crossway Books, 2008), 343.

2. Alister McGrath, *Doubting: Growing Through the Uncertainties of Faith* (Downers Grove, IL: InterVarsity Press, 2006), 121.

3. See chapter 10, "Doubt: How to Handle It," in McGrath's book *Doubting*.

4. See Genesis 6–8.

5. See Exodus 14.

6. See Exodus 16.

7. See Joshua 6.

8. See Daniel 3:8-30.

9. See Daniel 6.

10. See Numbers 22:21-41.

11. See Ezekiel 4.

12. See Judges 15:15. Note: Judges 15:14 reports that it was God's strength that rushed upon Samson, obviously making such a feat possible.

13. See 1 Samuel 17.

14. See Jonah 1:17.

15. See Acts 2:1-4.

16. Genesis 21:6.

17. Watch my video "How Do We Interpret the Seemingly Ridiculous?" at *The One Minute Apologist,* www.youtube.com/watch?v=VVENJAK5Z-Y.

18. See Genesis 22.

19. Hebrews 11:17-19.

20. McGrath, *Doubting,* 24-25.

21. J.P. Moreland, *Love Your God with All Your Mind* (Colorado Springs, CO: NavPress, 1997), 74, emphasis added.

22. See Ephesians 2:8-9.

23. Alexis de Tocqueville, *Democracy in America* (New York: Penguin Putnam, 2003), emphasis added.

24. 2 Corinthians 1:22.

25. Romans 8:16.

26. 2 Timothy 1:12, emphasis added.

27. 1 John 5:13, emphasis added.

28. The word *certainty* used in Luke 1:4 refers to the "stability of a statement." Luke has done his research. His account is *stable*. Trustworthy. In Acts 2:36 Luke uses the word again because he wants his readers to know *beyond a doubt*. That is his *desire,* understandably so, as it should be ours, but that doesn't mean we won't have questions. Furthermore, his account was fresh. After two thousand years of church history, today's believers have a lot of terrain to travel through, which often creates questions. Nevertheless, believers can know that Luke's account is stable and he desires followers of Christ to have certainty.

29. Hebrews 11:6.

30. Elie Wiesel, *Night* (New York: Farrar, Straus and Giroux, 2006), 34.

31. Ibid., 45.

32. See Habakkuk 1:2-4.

33. C.S. Lewis, *Mere Christianity* (New York: HarperCollins, 2001), 38.

34. Donald E. Gowan, *The Triumph of Faith in Habakkuk* (Eugene, OR: Wipf and Stock, 2009), 26.

35. Romans 1:20.

36. Genesis 18:25, emphasis added.

37. Richard Dawkins, *The God Delusion* (New York: Houghton Mifflin, 2006).

Chapter 5: Doubt Triggers: Part 2

1. Quote taken from the cover of Bart D. Ehrman, *Jesus, Interrupted* (New York: HarperOne, 2009).

2. Ehrman, *Jesus, Interrupted*, 10.

3. Ibid., 7.

4. Ibid., 8.

5. Ibid., 7.

6. Ibid., 6.

7. Norman Geisler and Thomas Howe, *When Critics Ask: A Popular Handbook on Bible Difficulties* (Grand Rapids, MI: Baker Books, 1992), 15-26.

8. Craig L. Blomberg, *Can We Still Believe the Bible?* (Grand Rapids, MI: Brazos Press, 2014), 1.

9. Ibid., 2.

10. To equip yourself further, add the following books to your personal library:

    • Gleason Archer. *New International Encyclopedia of Bible Difficulties*. Zondervan, 2001.

    • William Arndt. *Does the Bible Contradict Itself? A Discussion of Alleged Contradictions of the Bible*. 5th rev. ed. Concordia, 1976.

    • Craig Blomberg. *Can We Still Believe The Bible? An Evangelical Engagement with Contemporary Questions*. Brazos Press, 2014, and his book *The Historical Reliability of the Gospels*. InterVarsity Press, 1987.

    • Norman Geisler and Thomas Howe. *When Critics Ask: A Popular Handbook on Bible Difficulties*. Baker Books, 1992.

    • Walter Kaiser et al. *Hard Sayings of the Bible*. InterVarsity Press, 1996.

- Andreas J. Köstenberger, Darrell L. Bock, and Josh D. Chatraw. *Truth in a Culture of Doubt: Engaging Skeptical Challenges to the Bible.* B&H Academic, 2014.

11. Darrell Bock's chapter titled "The Words of Jesus in the Gospels: Live, Jive, or Memorex" in the book *Jesus Under Fire* (Grand Rapids, MI: Zondervan, 1995) was pivotal in helping me to walk out of my synoptic doubt crisis.

12. Bart D. Ehrman, *God's Problem: How the Bible Fails to Answer Our Most Important Question—Why We Suffer* (New York: HarperCollins, 2008), 3-4.

13. N.T. Wright, *Evil and the Justice of God* (Downers Grove, IL: InterVarsity Press, 2006), 41.

14. Hebrews 3:12-14.

15. Mark 12:30.

16. Jeremiah 29:13.

17. Luke 11:1.

18. Habakkuk 1:2.

19. Matthew 28:20.

Chapter 6: Four Facets of Doubt

1. 1 Peter 3:7.

2. I'm thankful to Gary Habermas for his work on doubt that first exposed me to some of the different types of doubt that we encounter. The book I'm referring to is *The Thomas Factor: Using Your Doubts to Draw Closer to God* (Nashville, TN: Broadman and Holman Publishers, 1999).

3. As a side note, each of the sub-emotions that we discussed can serve as primary emotions at certain times in our life. When emotional doubt is our biggest crisis, it's important to do a little exploratory work to get beneath our doubt. However, when anger is our primary emotion, we may find that doubt serves as a sub-emotion to our anger. For instance, we may be angry because we doubt that God cares for us. So it's a little tricky at times to understand ourselves emotionally. But it's a project we cannot afford to ignore, especially when life inflicts us.

4. I extracted this example from a DVD series I produced with William Lane Craig concerning his book *On Guard.* (Colorado Springs, CO: David C. Cook, 2010). To learn more visit http://apps.biola.edu/apologetics-store/products/special-discounted-sets-or-combos/item/on-guard-defending-your-faith-with-reason-and-precision-box-set.

5. 1 John 3:8.

6. Romans 5:3-4.

7. Walter Kaiser, *The Old Testament Documents: Are They Reliable and Relevant?* (Downers Grove, IL: InterVarsity Press, 2001), 24.

8. Ibid.

9. A simple yet helpful read is the book by Howard Hendricks and William Hendricks, *Living by the Book* (Chicago: Moody Publishers, 2007). This book will show you how to be a faithful student of Scripture. Every Christian should read at least one book on how to study the Bible. Another book worth reading is Gordon Fee and Douglas Stuart's *How to Read the Bible for All Its Worth,* 4th ed. (Grand Rapids, MI: Zondervan, 2014).

10. Luke 22:42.

11. Matthew 6:10.

12. Philippians 2:12-13; 4:13.

13. Romans 12:1.

14. For example, see John 20:31; 2 Timothy 1:12.

15. Psalm 19:1.

16. Romans 1:19-20, emphasis added.

17. 1 Corinthians 15:14.

18. For instance, see Matthew 5:17-18; 23:35; Luke 24:27; John 10:35; 14:26; 16:13.

Chapter 7: The Root of Doubt

1. 1 Peter 5:8.

2. Ephesians 6:12.

3. C.S. Lewis, *The Screwtape Letters* (New York: HarperCollins Publishers, 1961), ix.

4. 2 Corinthians 4:4.

5. John 8:44.

6. Matthew 4:3.

7. Revelation 12:9.

8. Revelation 20:10.

9. Genesis 3:1 NASB. The Genesis account doesn't identify the serpent as Satan, but the book of Revelation clearly associates the ancient serpent with the devil or Satan (see Revelation 12:9; 20:2).

10. Genesis 3:1-7.

11. Bruce K. Waltke with Cathi J. Fredricks, *Genesis: A Commentary* (Grand Rapids, MI: Zondervan, 2001), 90.

12. 2 Corinthians 11:14.

13. Richard Baxter, *The Reformed Pastor*, 74-75, emphasis added.

14. For example, see 1 Thessalonians 4:16-17.

15. Genesis 3:4-5.

16. Genesis 2:15-17.

17. Genesis 3:6.

18. Genesis 3:6.

19. Genesis 3:7.

20. Sheldon Vanauken, *A Severe Mercy* (San Francisco: Harper and Row, 1977), 99.

21. Matthew 4:1-11.

22. Luke 22:31.

23. Luke 22:32, emphasis added.

24. Mark 14:31.

25. 1 Corinthians 10:12 NIV.

26. Ephesians 6:13.

27. Ephesians 6:16, emphasis added.

28. See Romans 8:34 and Hebrews 7:25.

29. Genesis 3:15.

30. James 4:7.

31. 1 John 4:4.

Chapter 8: Navigating Doubt

1. Jude 22.

2. 1 Corinthians 13:12, emphasis added.

3. Alister E. McGrath, *Doubting: Growing Through the Uncertainties of Faith* (Downers Grove, IL: InterVarsity Press, 2006), 121.

4. Jennifer Michael Hecht, *Doubt: A History* (New York: HarperCollins, 2003), xvi.

5. "Quotes about Spiritual Leadership," *Goodreads*, www.goodreads.com/quotes/tag/spiritual-leadership.

6. 1 Thessalonians 5:21.

7. 1 John 4:1.

8. Philippians 1:9-10, emphasis added.

9. James 1:5.

10. See Ephesians 4:11-12.

11. Ephesians 4:14.

12. Psalm 145:18, emphasis added.

13. Isaiah 1:18.

14. Jeremiah 29:13-14, emphasis added.

15. Psalm 13.

16. Psalm 77:10, emphasis added.

17. Deuteronomy 5:15. See also Deuteronomy 15:15; 16:12; 24:18,22.

18. Matthew 14:31, emphasis added.

19. Isaiah 26:3.

20. C. Stephen Evans and R. Zachary Manis, *Philosophy of Religion,* 2nd ed. (Downers Grove, IL: InterVarsity Press, 2009), 209.

21. Ibid., 208.

22. John 7:17, emphasis added.

23. See Luke 1:46-55.

24. For a good resource on fasting, get a copy of John Piper's book *A Hunger for God* (Wheaton, IL: Crossway Books, 2013).

Chapter 9: Faith Defined

1. Hebrews 11:6, emphasis added.

2. See Matthew 17:20. Here Jesus likens faith that has amazing effectiveness to something as small as a mustard seed.

3. Steven Pinker, "Less Faith, More Reason," *The Harvard Crimson,* October 27, 2006; www.thecrimson.com/article/2006/10/27/less-faith-more-reason-there-is/.

4. www.goodreads.com/quotes/46350-faith-is-the-great-cop-out-the-great-excuse-to-evade.

5. Richard Dawkins, *The God Delusion* (New York: Houghton Mifflin, 2006), 308.

6. Sam Harris, *Letter to a Christian Nation* (New York: Alfred A. Knopf, 2006), 110.

7. 1 Corinthians 15:17.

8. Consider the empty tomb, Jesus's postresurrection appearances, and the transformation of the disciples who could hardly follow Him during His earthly ministry. Furthermore, how do you explain the birth of the church apart from the resurrection?

9. Lee Strobel, "How Easter Killed My Faith in Atheism," *Room for Doubt*, www.roomfordoubt. com/examine/1/Stories-of-Doubt/44/How-Easter-Killed-My-Faith-in-Atheism.

10. Ravi Zacharias, *Jesus Among Other Gods: The Absolute Claims of the Christian Message* (Nashville, TN: Thomas Nelson, 2000), 146.

11. See Proverbs 1:7.

12. William Lane Craig, "Faith and Doubt," *Reasonable Faith*, www.reasonablefaith.org/faith-and-doubt#ixzz31AKbsb2d.

13. *Cambridge Dictionaries Online*, http://dictionary.cambridge.org/us/dictionary/american-english/faith.

14. See Matthew 8:26; 15:28; Luke 7:9; 17:6.

15. Emily Dickinson, *Selected Letters*, ed. Thomas H. Johnson (Cambridge, MA: Harvard University Press, 1986), 279.

16. J.P. Moreland and Klaus Issler, *In Search of a Confident Faith: Overcoming Barriers to Trusting in God* (Downers Grove, IL: InterVarsity Press, 2008), 18.

17. Ibid., 25.

18. I believe Moreland and Issler make a great point, even though the word *faith* is in the title of my book and it's what I'm aiming you toward. In the end, *faith* is still a biblical word and it warrants proper explanation, but to use replacement words in your conversations may be very wise as *faith* has indeed become a loaded and often misunderstood word.

19. Hebrews 11:1, emphasis added.

20. Building on this argument that faith is more like confidence, Moreland and Issler note:

> Once we recognize that faith is confidence or trust, it is easier to understand why there have been three standard parts of faith regularly taken throughout church history (especially during the Reformation) to flesh out the relevant biblical teaching—faith as knowledge *(notitia)*, faith as assent *(assensus)* and faith as commitment *(fiducia)*. *Notitia* refers to the content of faith, primarily the assertions of Scripture and theological, doctrinal formulations derived from Scripture…*Notitia* is also defined as knowledge of the meaning of or as understanding the content of doctrinal teaching. This clearly implies that far from being antithetical to faith, knowledge is actually an important ingredient of it…*Assensus* refers to personal assent to, awareness of or agreement with the truth of Christian teaching, and, again, it is primarily intellectual…The important thing is that it is not enough to *grasp* the contents of Christian teaching; one must also *accept* the fact that this teaching is true…Finally, *fiducia* involves personal commitment to its object, whether to a truth or a person. *Fiducia* is essentially a matter of the will, but because Christianity is a relationship with a Person and not just commitment to a set of truths (though this is, of course, essential), the

capacity to develop emotional intimacy and to discern the inner movements of feeling, intuition and God's Spirit in the soul is crucial to maintaining and cultivating commitment to God…These three classical distinctions—*noticia, assensus* and *fiducia*—are indispensable to helping us build a broader understanding of the concept of faith. (Moreland and Issler, *In Search of Confident Faith*, 19-22.)

Chapter 10: *Toward* Faith

1. G.K. Chesterton, *Orthodoxy* (Colorado Springs, CO: Image Classics, 1991), 23.

2. Romans 1:17.

3. Galatians 3:11.

4. Hebrews 10:38.

5. Habakkuk 2:4.

6. 2 Corinthians 5:7.

7. Ephesians 2:8a, emphasis added.

8. Romans 4:20-21.

9. See also 2 Corinthians 10:15 for another text that proves our faith can increase.

10. Romans 10:17.

11. 1 Thessalonians 3:6-7.

12. Ephesians 6:16.

13. Hebrews 13:7.

14. James 1:3.

15. James 1:6-8.

16. 1 Peter 1:6-9.

17. 1 John 5:4-5.

18. Jude 3-4.

19. Luke 18:8.

20. Philip Yancey, *Reaching for the Invisible God* (Grand Rapids, MI: Zondervan, 2000), 42.

21. Isaiah 7:9.

22. 1 Corinthians 13:12.

23. Romans 8:16.

24. Read William Lane Craig's answer to his "Question of the Week" regarding "The Witness of the Holy Spirit" at www.reasonablefaith.org/the-witness-of-the-holy-spirit.

25. *Weltschmerz* is a German word that literally means "world pain." It can refer to a skeptically based nihilistic loathing and desperation.

26. 1 John 5:13, emphasis added.

27. To help you in this endeavor, I encourage you to read Gary Habermas's book *The Thomas Factor*. In it he discusses different species of doubt and offers powerful solutions for tackling your doubts. Also, during some personal correspondence with Gary regarding doubt, he highly recommended *Telling Yourself the Truth* by William Backus and Marie Chapian: "In my opinion, it is the best popular volume on controlling some of the worst emotional pain in our lives. The book takes the reader, step-by-step, through a fairly simple, straightforward three-step process

that Backus and Chapian say has proven to work very well in a high percentage of cases (well over 90 percent were helped, according to their tests). So if you want to get a handle on the pain of your doubt, Backus and Chapian have probably influenced me more than any other book that I have ever read in my entire life, on any subject (!), besides only the Bible...I cannot recommend the Backus and Chapian book highly enough."

28. 2 Corinthians 10:5.

29. Billy Graham, *Just As I Am: The Autobiography of Billy Graham* (New York: HarperCollins, 1997), 135.

30. Ibid., 138-39.

About the Author

Bobby Conway is lead pastor of Life Fellowship Church near Charlotte, NC. He is a graduate of Dallas Theological Seminary (ThM), Southern Evangelical Seminary (DMin), and is a PhD candidate in the philosophy of religion department at the University of Birmingham (UK). Bobby is the author of *The Fifth Gospel* and *Hell, Rob Bell, and What Happens When People Die?* and also the founder and host of the *One Minute Apologist* (www.oneminuteapologist.com). In addition, he and his wife, Heather, serve on the Family Life "Weekend to Remember" marriage conference speaking team. His hobbies include date nights with his bride, family time with his kids, traveling, and reading lots of books many people would describe as boring.

Also by Bobby Conway

The Fifth Gospel
Matthew, Mark, Luke, John...You

"There are five Gospels: Matthew, Mark, Luke, John...and the Christian. But most people never read the first four."

There are any number of books on how to *do* evangelism. This book is different—it's an invitation to actually *live out* the message of the gospel. Jesus's original intention was for ordinary people like you and me to live lives that point others to the only Person who can give them hope for this life as well as the next—to visibly display the Good News of salvation through the Messiah and Redeemer of humankind.

But many Christ followers today are either ridden with guilt for not telling others about Jesus or so silent that no one really knows they're a Christian. *The Fifth Gospel* will help you wrestle with the critical issues involved in living out your faith in front of a watching and sometimes not-so-friendly world.

Isn't it time to become a witness for the One you profess to love? Prepare yourself to represent your Savior well and to discover a new way to do evangelism. Get ready for God to unleash the gospel through you!

To learn more about Harvest House books and
to read sample chapters, visit our website:

www.harvesthousepublishers.com

HARVEST HOUSE PUBLISHERS
EUGENE, OREGON